The Road to Transylvania

A Family Adventure

Phil & Elaine Slade

Boz Publications Ltd.
71-75 Shelton Street - Covent Garden - London - WC2H 9JQ - UK.
office@bozpublications.com / www.bozpublications.com

Copyright © 2020 Slade's Books
First published 2016 by Phil Slade
Revised edition 2020 by Boz Publications Ltd

The right of Elaine and Phil Slade to be identified as the author of this work has been asserted by them in accordance with the Copyright, Designs and Patents Act 1988.

All rights reserved. No part of this publication may be reproduced, stored in a retrieval system, or transmitted in any other form or by any means, electronic, mechanical, photocopying, recording or otherwise, without the prior written permission of the authors.
Permissions may be obtained by writing to the authors at: office@bozpublications.com

ISBN: 978-1-9164216-5-3

Cover Photo by Matt Fleming
Pictures of Keresztur and Udvarhely by Fazakas Bence
New International Version (NIV) Copyright © 1973, 1978, 1984, 2011 by Biblica.

A CIP catalogue record for this book is available from the British Library.

Dedicated to Kerry Anne Stephens.

Kerry was a faithful friend and became part of our family throughout our life in London and Cobham. She saw serving our family as part of her calling alongside her nursing career. Kerry supported us fully in the ten years of Phil's social action business. Sadly she died in 2015 having suffered two brain tumours.

CONTENTS

Acknowledgements	6
Recommendations	7
Foreword	11
Introduction	19

PART ONE
(Our Story)

A Move To Cobham	25
A Call To Romania?	29
Was It A Call?	33
Working Through The Call	37
God Is A God Of Miracles	43
Moving To Romania	47
Baptism Of Ice	53
Székelykeresztúr/Cristuru Secuiesc	57
Continued Support And Education	61
Székelyudvarhely/Odorheiu Secuiesc	65
Missing Home And Some Answers	71
Children's Home Closing	79
Phil's Father And Family	81
Drinking Water And Food	85
Third Year	89
Supporting The Young People	93
End Of The Third Year	97
Craft Romania And Fair Trade (CRAFT UK)	105
Closure Of The Business And Sztoika Csaba	117

PART TWO
(Perspectives)

Elaine	125
Anne	135
Rachel	141
Becky	149
Abi	159
Sztoika Csaba	165
Paul Knowlson	167
Bodrogi Csaba	173
Fazakas István (Pisti)	177
Bodrogi Lehel	181
Tim Poole	183
Things We Have Learnt	189
Epilogue	195

ACKNOWLEDGEMENTS

My thanks go to my family, who stood by me as I took time out over two years to write the first edition.

To my wife who had urged me to record our story to encourage others. Also, my good friend Bodrogi Csaba who said I should write all the things down that God has done through our journey, put it in a book and have it published.

To the many people who have proofread and suggested improvements, including my wife Elaine and Rev. Charles May (my father-in-law), S-P O'Mahoney, Lucy Greenland and Meg Miller who have gone through the draft with a fine toothcomb.

To family and friends that have contributed to this book, including Elaine, Anne, Rachel, Becky and Abi. Bodrogi Csaba, Bodrogi Lehel, Steve Clifford, Sztoika Csaba, Fazakas István, Paul Knowlson, Rev. Charles May, Tim Poole, Matthew Skirton, Stefan Loránd and to Linda Harding and David Taylor who have written a foreword to the book. Elaine has joined me in co-authoring this second edition.

To Andy Smithyman who has guided me and put in a lot of time in getting this second edition to print.

A special thanks to Her Majesty Margareta of Romania, Custodian of the Romanian Crown for such kind words about this book.

RECOMMENDATIONS

The Slade family heard God's call and set off, by faith, into the unknown. They were willing to uproot their family and cross geographical and cultural barriers because they knew how important it was to share their love of Jesus with those who were yet to hear of and experience his love. The way the whole family were included in the decision to go and the ministry that followed is a great example for families who are considering following Jesus' Great Commission to, "Go and make disciples of all nations." I recommend this book to all who, recognising God's call to witness to all peoples, are asking, "What would it mean for me and my family to leave the comforts and familiarities of my own country and serve as a cross cultural missionary?"

Matthew Skirton, OM UK CEO.

The Road to Transylvania tells the inspirational story of a whole family's obedient response to God's call on their lives. The book provides us with a fascinating blow by blow account of the practical, relational and spiritual journey from suburban Surrey to live in a small Romanian town; how they expressed the love of God particularly to young people, many of whom had lived in a now infamous state-run orphanage.

Steve Clifford Christian Leader, Speaker and Author.
Former General Director of the UK Evangelical Alliance.

Phil Slade and his family packed themselves up and moved from the UK to Transylvania motivated by a love for Romania. This book captures their adventures and is an example to us all of beautiful things that happen when we follow our calling, however disruptive that may seem at first glance.

Her Majesty Margareta of Romania, Custodian of the Romanian Crown.

THE ROAD TO TRANSYLVANIA

FOREWORD

I doubt there could be anyone more qualified to write the forewords to this book. Linda Harding has been a great friend and support to all our family in our journey, with advice and prayer. David Taylor has also been a great friend and support from the time he was involved in sending us out. His wife has been a colleague and friend of Elaine's on the Leadership team at St Andrew's School.

Linda Harding was a church leader in Cobham. After an NHS career as a Speech Therapist and then a manager, she pursued her childhood dream of going to the nations. Since 1999 Linda has been mentoring people in cross-cultural mission, introduced a mobilising tool "Kairos' in 50 countries and served as European director for "World Outreach International" until passing the baton to the next generation and retiring from formal responsibilities. Linda now devotes her time to visiting missionaries and encouraging people to live as a blessing to all nations.

I am delighted to contribute to the Foreword to this book. This family are a remarkable family, and I thank God for being part of their lives.

Over the years, many young (and a few older) people made the journey from leafy Cobham to Romania. For many like Anne, and later Phil, and then the rest of the family, it was a pivotal and transformative point in their life. This inspiring and heart-rending story tells how this family responded to God's invitation to live sacrificially for others and to be a family for so many young people, a lifestyle that continues today. It is a story that needs to be told and one that will challenge its readers as they read of one family's faithfulness in answering God's call to live in Romania.

My earliest memory of the Slade family was when Phil and Elaine, soon after they and the four girls arrived in Cobham, got involved with leading a discipleship group for children 9-11 years old. They worked with me in the church children's work leadership team. What a blessing they were. When Phil dreamed of an initiative called Buzz, this further demonstrated his, and Elaine's, passion for seeing the next generation of youth and children loved, mentored and equipped.

This passion was tested and implemented when Anne, at age 14, went to Romania for two weeks. The poverty she witnessed impacted her, and she longed to help there in the future. I vividly remember Anne taking me up to her bedroom and talking me through the stories of the children whose photos were plastered all over her walls and ceiling!

Then came Phil's visit, where he knew God was calling him to take his family to Romania, and the family visit there in the summer of 1999. I remember them recounting the day when they were first exposed to the appalling scenes in Romania.

It was a personal challenge for me to continue to walk closely with them in their journey of pursuing Gods call to Romania; I was at the same time pursuing God's call to me to live in Japan. A test of this family's courage and determination for God's heart for the broken-hearted was when they agreed that same year for Rachel and Becky to visit me in Japan - at the ages of 15 and 11! To set in context, Becky had initiated and led a weekly prayer group for me in Japan, with her school friends. Phil and Elaine were willing to let their girls go halfway around the world to spend half term with me. Amazing!

FOREWORD

My first and only visit to the Slade's home in Odorheiu Secuiesc was memorable. They were living the life as an inclusive family in their distinctive way - warmly welcoming and loving many young people into their home and hearts. One weekend, I joined in with thirty of their family round the Sunday lunch table. There was always enough food and love.

This is truly a family story, and the insights by Anne, Rachel, Becky and Abi are very moving. I commend to you to read the lessons learnt in this story - they are deeply insightful. If you want to stay comfortable, don't join the Slade family in their life journey.

This is a story of life on the edge, an adventure of God's provision and protection. It is inspiring to read how God spoke to each one of the girls as well as to Phil and Elaine. This sense of individual call was pivotal to this story and without that agreement this story would not be told. I marvel at the grace and understanding God gave to each of the girls to share their Mum and Dad with up to 200 others, and the capacity God gave and still gives to Phil and Elaine to love so many children. But it was not easy, and there was much sacrifice and heartbreak.

I love their fruitful stories and their brutal honesty - their ability to articulate lessons learned, with humility and clarity. I love their example of following the finger of God, and I love their passion to just be what God has called them to be. The Slade family will always have a special place in my heart.

> *David Taylor founded the Charity Cobham Romania Aid in 1990, which became Heart for Romania (HfR). He was also founder of the Fundatia, Heart for Romania in Romania. He, along with Chris Williamson were part of the team sending us out to Romania. He is a Lawyer by Profession. He is also a Historian and Writer. He was Director of the Princess Margarita of Romania Foundation for several years and a fundraiser with the Hospice of Hope building, Romania's first hospice in Brașov.*

I am delighted to contribute to the Foreword to this book. It is a story that needs to be told and which will inspire and challenge its readers as they read of the Slade family's faithfulness in answering God's call to live in Romania. I have been asked to set the Slade's story in context, and so I hope that what follows will do that.

In late 1989 communism collapsed in Eastern Europe as the Berlin Wall came down and thousands of people from East Germany began to pour across the former boundary into the West. These were truly remarkable days, and I well remember one elderly person saying that for him this was the real end of the Second World War. It was not long after that we witnessed on our television screens further remarkable scenes from Bucharest, the capital city of Romania, as the evil dictator Nicolae Ceausescu who had had such a strong hold on his country was booed and jeered by the crowds who had gathered to hear him speak. Events quickly unfolded as Ceausescu was hustled away by his bodyguards to be flown by helicopter to what he hoped was a safe place. However, he was soon apprehended, taken for trial and promptly executed. All of this took place before the eyes of the world and was relayed into homes by the media as events took place.

I have lived all my life in Cobham and have had a passion for history since my childhood years. When I saw these events take place, I really sensed that I was witnessing historic events of a magnitude not seen since the end of World War II. I longed to go and witness these events for myself but realised that was quite impossible. However, it seemed that God had other plans.

Just a few weeks later, I attended a church event in Tolworth where Danny Smith, from Jubilee Church, was to speak about what was happening in Eastern Europe from a Christian perspective and how we as churches and individuals might get involved. As I drove to that meeting, I can honestly say I felt as never before God saying that it was to be an important day in my life. Danny spoke of the work that his organisation had undertaken in secret over many years by taking Bibles into countries behind the Iron Curtain. Turning to current events, he said how the biggest needs were now in Romania which had suddenly opened its borders. As aid was allowed in, suddenly there appeared the most shocking images of thousands of unwanted children who had been put into Homes in the most appalling conditions. Those images began to find their way on to the front pages of our newspapers and very soon many people in the UK and elsewhere were filling cars and vans with humanitarian aid and setting off to Romania.

As Danny Smith told his stories of the shocking scenes in Romania, he called for volunteers to come forward and join organised teams that were going to Romania. It was then that I felt, "This is it!" However, as I was a leader in a large house church with many resources, I felt that rather than just offer my own services, I should volunteer a team. I spoke with a fellow leader and we agreed to do just this.

After returning to Cobham, I was given the task of bringing together a team who could travel 2000 miles across Europe to bring practical aid to Romania. Jubilee Church provided us with the name of one particular Children's Home and plans for some specific work required in terms of a new washroom.

Through my existing community links in Cobham, we were able to raise finances, hire vans, and collect food and the other recourses needed for the job. When we eventually left for Romania, we were given a send-off by our local MP, the leader of Surrey County Council, and many others from our local community. The journey took several days as we crossed borders and slept in church halls and other places on our way.

Eventually, we arrived in Romania and found our way to the small town of Cristuru Secuiesc, (the Place of the Lord's Cross). It was dark when we arrived at the children's home which turned out to be one of the largest in Romania. In England we had, with difficulty, found some Romanian phrasebooks. However, as we began to explain to the Director who we were, we discovered that we were actually in a Hungarian speaking part of Romania and that our phrasebooks were of little use!

We spent that night and several more sleeping on the floor, as we set about refurbishing a washroom used by hundreds of children. It was in an appalling state. Water just ran everywhere, and the toilets were blocked with excrement. The smell was unbelievable. However, we undertook the task given to us and eventually returned to England.

Upon returning, we realised that we could not leave things as they were. Further visits took place as we built up an ongoing relationship with the staff, the children, and the people of Cristuru Secuiesc. We eventually established Cobham Romania Aid which worked to raise funds to continue the work and deepen the links in Romania. We had widespread community support both in and outside of the churches.

Over the years, many young (and a few older) people made the journey to Romania. For many like Phil and Elaine Slade, it was a seminal point in their life. One member of an early team now holds a responsible post with the United Nations.

The motto for Cobham Romania Aid (after Heart for Romania) is, 'Hope, Help and Heart.' The Slade family have most certainly brought all those things to the people they have met and lived with. This book is a timely account of how one family responded to God's call to head to Transylvania. In recognising their contribution to this important chapter in the work of Heart for Romania, I would also like to express my thanks to those who joined me on that very first trip and whose team photograph still sits before me on desk. Sadly, Ralph Somerville is now with God. His practical skills in those early days were invaluable. The others on that first team were Simon Ball, Gordon (now Jack) Henderson, Nick Perrott, Richard Ramsden, David Skinner, Chris Williamson and Paul Wood. They laid a foundation on which so many others like the Slade family have, and are continuing, to build.

THE ROAD TO TRANSYLVANIA

INTRODUCTION

What is the purpose of this book? Many people have said we should write down the experiences related to our journey as a family. The purposes are threefold.

1. To give glory to God. We are humbled by the words that people have written about us in this book. All we did as a family was to follow God's path and allow Him to use our natural talents as a channel through which He could speak to others. The rest was up to Him; we had the deep privilege of watching Him take over in the most difficult of situations. It could happen for you too.
2. To be a book people can refer to when they believe they have a call to go but wonder how it could affect their family.
3. A book that suggests lessons that we learnt as an English family living in Romania.

In this book you may ask yourself, "Why did the Slade family move to Romania and then learn Hungarian?" The reason is that we moved to a predominantly Hungarian speaking region *(see image on page 21)*. This map will also help you trace the places mentioned throughout our various adventures. Throughout the book, the names of towns and villages in the areas that we lived and worked are referred to in both Hungarian and Romanian.

Some names of those mentioned in the book whose childhood started in the Children's Home have been changed for personal reasons.

A BRIEF HISTORY OF THE AREA

Székelyudvarhely was an administrative county (comitatus) of the Kingdom of Hungary. Its territory is now in central Romania (eastern Transylvania). The capital of the county was Székelyudvarhely (with a Romanian name of Odorheiu Secuiesc).

The Székelyudvarhely region was a settlement (seat) of the Székely. In the Middle Ages, the Székelys, along with the Transylvanian Saxons, played a key role in the defence of the Kingdom of Hungary against the Ottomans in their posture as guards of the eastern border. With the Treaty of Trianon of 1920, Transylvania (including the Székely Land) became part of Romania except during the Hungarian occupation between 1940–1944 during World War II.

In post-Cold War Romania, the Székelys formed roughly half of the ethnic Hungarian population. They were estimated to number about eight hundred and sixty thousand in the 1970s and are officially recognised as a distinct minority group by the Romanian government.

Udvarhelyszék, Udvarhely County was formed in 1876, when the administrative structure of Transylvania was changed. Its territory constitutes now the present Romanian county of Harghita, It was made up of around ninety-six percent of people where their first language was Hungarian.

INTRODUCTION

THE HARGHITA REGION OF ROMANIA

Image by Andrei Nacu (adapted)

THE ROAD TO TRANSYLVANIA

PART ONE

Our Story

THE ROAD TO TRANSYLVANIA

CHAPTER 1

A MOVE TO COBHAM

Having lived in East London long before Elaine and Phil were married, a move to Surrey seemed like a step into a slower leafy village life away from the busy, bustling City. Our girls remember going into London late at night to see the Christmas lights in Oxford Street and taking many a stroll along the River Thames together. Anne, our eldest daughter, remembers these exciting adventures well and has fond memories of looking up at the green windows of County Hall and feeling proud that her daddy worked there. Often Elaine would bundle the girls into the car in their pyjamas, after getting them ready for bed, to come and pick Phil up from work.

We had brought up our four girls in Hackney. Elaine was teaching Infants in Primary schools and leading worship in St Luke's Church Hackney, and we both led a Home Group. Phil was churchwarden and Youth co-ordinator as well as having a demanding job as Direct Labour Manager of Grounds Maintenance for all the schools in the Inner London Education Authority, with a workforce of around two hundred and fifty people. In the final year before moving to Cobham, he was Head of Grounds Maintenance for ILEA which included all the school playing fields and outer County sites as well as the school grounds. In 1990, Phil was made redundant from ILEA. It was the push we needed to get out of our comfort zone and down the A3 to Cobham.

This was very much a time of change, and we knew we both needed to slow down and see what God had for us on our next part of the journey. Elaine first worked at St Andrew's Oxshott Playgroup for four years before accepting a teaching post at St Andrew's School in Cobham. Phil went back to his horticultural roots and looked after the grounds of Fairmile Court; within a short time, he became General Maintenance Manager and finally responsible for the entire Conference Centre when the previous Manager left. A decision to sell Fairmile Court by its owners, the Great St Helen's Church in the City of London, came after a terrorist bombing in 1992 destroyed part of the church building. Money allocated to upgrade Fairmile Court to modern standards was diverted to rebuild the church. Thus, Phil was redundant for the third time in his life. For a while, he worked for Octagon Homes who were the Developers for the Fairmile Court site.

Since moving to Cobham, we had looked at various churches with a view to attending one of them. We finally decided on Cobham Christian Fellowship, led by Gerald Coates, as it was very much part of the community at that time (CCF later became Pioneer People). We started getting involved in the life of the church, leading an Acorn group for children 9-11 years old; Phil then became the overall leader for the Acorn groups which flourished. Both Elaine and Phil were included in the leadership team for children's work, set up by Linda Harding. From this came several new initiatives such as Trail Blazers and then later Buzz.

Buzz became an amazing initiative, stemming from Phil's passion for seeing the next generation of youth and children equipped and mentored, enabling them to exercise their gifts in real situations. It emanated from an idea that Phil had of asking Noel Richards, a nationally well-known worship leader from Pioneer People, to put on a Cobham-based event similar to the event Noel was putting on at Wembley Stadium called, Champion of the World. The difference was that the children of Pioneer People would host and lead through the event and ask their friends to come. The event was a resounding success and the children asked if they could continue the events, which they did at St Andrew's school for over a year. Other local churches soon heard about it and came to observe and ask questions. They asked us to consider hosting such events in their local schools, and this evolved into, Buzz on The Road.

The Buzz team consisted of a group of adults who were all committed to mentoring young people with similar gifts to their own; for example, Elaine mentored those with worship gifts, Phil mentored overall event management. Buzz on The Road was very successful, and we regularly toured around five other schools for two years.

With Fairmile Court closed, Phil was asked to consider taking on the role of Maintenance Manager at the Proclamation Trust (connected to St Helen's in London) at their Headquarters in Borough High Street. This involved commuting back to London every day with responsibilities for a four-floor office building close to London Bridge and maintenance of other sites they owned. Strangely enough, he became responsible for maintaining the lease and maintenance contract to one of the largest basket wholesalers at that time who rented our lower floor as a showroom and offices. Was this the start of being interested in willow baskets?

THE ROAD TO TRANSYLVANIA

CHAPTER 2

A CALL TO ROMANIA?

Our girls were growing up; they were at various stages of education either at St Andrew's Primary school, Cobham where Elaine taught or at Therfield, the secondary school in Leatherhead. Anne, our eldest was 14, Rachel 12, Becky 8, and Abi 6 years old respectively. Pioneer People had a history of being involved in the Transylvanian region of Romania since the Revolution in 1990.

David Taylor, who was the Founder of Cobham Romania Aid, had been involved as had many others from the community of Cobham, in practically repairing a large orphanage in the village of Cristuru Secuiesc (Székelykeresztúr in Hungarian). As a family, we attended an event called Event without Walls put on by Pioneer in 1995 at Exeter Showground. Phil was asked by Alan Moore to help by supporting him in some of the manual tasks. Alan had been one of the first to go to Romania, and we discussed what it had been like there. Perhaps this sowed a seed in Phil's heart for God to water later on?

Cobham Romania Aid became, Heart for Romania (HfR) as its membership spread across a wider area of Surrey. HfR was regularly sending groups of young people out with adult leaders to run camps in the summer months in the Székelykeresztúr/ Cristuru Secuiesc region for the children from the Children's Home.

When Anne was 14 in 1996; Tim Poole (the Camps co-ordinator) asked us if she would like to join one of the teams. We were sure she wouldn't as she was such a home bird, but she surprised us with a positive response. She was away for two weeks and came back a very different girl. She had been impacted by the poverty and conditions that the people lived in there and had a passion for helping them in the future. After the second year of going to camp, in 1997, she returned and pleaded with Phil to go and see for himself what it was like. She told Phil he just had to go. He was so intrigued by her passion; he volunteered to go on a camp the following year with the proviso that he could get the time off with unpaid leave and that he would be a helper NOT a leader as he had so many other leadership roles that he was involved in at that time. God has a funny way of making things happen; Proclamation Trust gave me two weeks paid leave to go. So, Phil had no excuse. He had felt quite guilty at not volunteering as a leader as he knew they were needed, however, just two days before we went the assistant leader broke his leg and Phil was asked to replace him; okay Lord, he thought, 'I give in!'

Phil helped lead the team that summer. Anne was part of the team, and he was so impacted by the people and place that he knew God was calling us as a family to Romania. On that camp, Phil met Fulop, Istvan (Ösci) and Balazs Csaba, who have continued to be friends to this day. On the plane home he contemplated how he was going to tell the family. He was met at the airport by Elaine who asked him what it had been like; it was probably not the time to say what was on his mind but he could not contain myself and he said, "We are going to live in Romania." In retrospect, it might have been better to gradually drip-feed his thoughts, as Elaine's and the other girls' response was one of shock at the time.

Then followed a period of reflection and talking with people we trusted; HfR, church leaders and Laurie and Pippa (who were also going to live in Székelykeresztúr/Cristuru Secuiesc). We were met with varying responses; some encouraging, some diffident, some definitely discouraging. We mulled and prayed over it for a year; Phil was sure, Elaine was less certain, she hadn't experienced what Phil had, so we decided to take the whole family to Romania for one month the next summer. We offered to lead a camp for two weeks and then to have a holiday in that region for two weeks. It was make-or-break time for us; one thing we knew for sure, if we went the children weren't just tagging along; they had to decide it was the right thing for them as well.

We had a wonderful summer; it opened all our eyes to another way of life, but it wasn't all easy, there were highlights and low lights. In the second part of the holiday we stayed at the Vadrozsa in Feliceni (Bikafalva), and whilst we were out swimming in their pool, a Hungarian man came to ask us if we were English. He had learned English himself and was keen to try his knowledge out. Within half an hour we were in his house, a few doors down from the motel and had met his family. We stayed for an evening meal and felt very welcome.

The highlight of the evening must have been when Csaba offered us a bowl of something Hungarian and delicious and asked if we would like some 'garbage' instead of 'cabbage'. We were rolling around laughing, and he too joined us in the comedy of it all. This was one of the first divine connections for us in Romania; this family were to become a lifeline to us when we moved out there.

As we went home, we had much to think about. Elaine was still uncertain, but we continued to pray and try to push doors. Our conversations with Linda Harding helped. One particular discussion clinched it for Elaine. She asked Linda, "How can it be right if it is just Phil that feels the connection with Romania or do, I say yes on the strength of what he feels?" Linda asked her, "What has God put on your heart?" Elaine replied, "Broken-hearted children." Linda laughed and said, "Well there you are then, who will you be dealing with most in Romania?" of course the answer was *broken-hearted children*.

So, Elaine and Phil were now in agreement that we should go; but it was hard to get the church leaders to listen. If we went, we would need to be sponsored mostly by the church and also by HfR; family and friends would make up the remainder. The church had not done this before; it would be a new model which was why it took so long to get a response. It was tough not to be listened to, to be discouraged and in November 1999 we decided to lay the Romania dream down. Despite letters to HfR and other church leaders, we were no further forward; we felt fourteen months of getting nowhere were enough, we had to put it on hold and if God wanted it to happen, He would have to resurrect it.

CHAPTER 3

WAS IT A CALL?

In February 2000 Phil was offered full-time work at Proclamation Trust; maybe Elaine could now go part-time as she had wanted to, the only drawback was that the money he was being offered would not equal what Elaine was being paid full-time. It wasn't enough for a growing family. Elaine felt it right that both of us went on the Pioneer Leader's Conference. She had asked God that He would speak to us in the next month about jobs. Our prayers were answered to a greater extent than she could have imagined. We arrived at the conference but were late for the first meeting. Elaine was greatly struck by Isaiah 54:2-3 which Gerald Coates (the Founder of the Pioneer churches) read:

> Enlarge the place of your tent, stretch your tent curtains wide, do not hold back; lengthen your cords, strengthen your stakes. For you will spread out to the right and to the left; your descendants will dispossess nations and settle in their desolate cities.

Enlarge your tents - what did this mean? Back in the chalet Elaine looked it up in her Bible, as she did so a piece of paper fell out on which she had written, "Phil, is Isaiah 54:2-3 suitable?"

She then turned to Isaiah in her Bible to find notes she had made for a pre-camp meeting the year before in June 1999 when she had been asked to lead a prayer time with those going out to camps in Romania that summer. "Were we ready to do things we didn't normally do?" she had written. Hmmm! What was God saying here?

The next morning at breakfast Chris Williamson, chair of HfR, sought us out and asked, "Are you serious about Romania? Do you know what you want to do out there?" We met him for lunch, and he asked us to put forward a working proposal for HfR to grapple with and to seek out advice from leaders on the weekend with us. We consulted all sorts of people we had connections with, and we trusted to be honest with us, and all were positive. Chris pursued us all day. "The only thing is" we told him, "We really wanted to go out this September (2000)." "A tight timescale" he replied, "but not impossible." Were we hearing him right? We then went to a session by Bill Wilson where he talked about stepping over that imaginary line- were we prepared to do it? He said, "The need is the Call." Well, we had seen the need in Romania! On the Sunday as we left, a close friend Jenny Moore said to us, "You'll be going!" We went home to talk to the girls; of course, they weren't shocked as they had heard this before, but they realised this time we were serious!

In the same week, Linda Harding came around for dinner; she encouraged us to go for it and would help in any way she could. We wrote the proposal by Friday and gave it to people we were accountable and to Linda to check before we handed it to Chris.

We gave the document in on Tuesday 29th February and specified that we needed to know by 31st March if we were to go this year, which by now would be a miracle in itself. We asked the Lord to close any wrong doors. Chris Williamson phoned us on Saturday 4th March and said HfR wanted us to meet with Pat Cook to test our call. She was a consultant that many Christian organisations used.

At the same time, we met with Mike and Lelonnie Hibberd, close friends from the Children's Leadership team who were going through a similar process. Mike said to us, "When you shut your eyes and dream, everything is possible, but when you open them the nightmare of reality sets in." This was helpful as we felt we were on such a roller coaster of emotions; excited one minute and scared stiff the next! We were one of the first pioneers, in a Pioneer church which had nothing in place to deal with this type of thing and we were forcing them to think about it.

We met with Pat Cook on Sunday 12th March. She talked to us and then to the whole family. Within minutes she said, "It is clear to me that you have a call, a long-term call." She was quite categorical and said she would strongly recommend us and that she would like to be part of our care when we went out. She was very supportive of the girls and they enjoyed her visit; on parting she gave us several things to look at.

THE ROAD TO TRANSYLVANIA

CHAPTER 4

WORKING THROUGH THE CALL

On the 14th March, we attended an HfR meeting in which we outlined our proposal and answered questions. We both discussed the possibility with our bosses and let them know there could be changes ahead. We researched home schooling for Becky and Abi and found although it was expensive, that it wasn't nearly as difficult as we first thought.

Laurie and Pippa phoned us from Romania on Friday 17th March. They talked about a three-bedroomed flat that was wonderfully furnished - what did we think? We weren't sure as we had asked God for a house, and Rachel had had a dream twice about a house out there.

We had been waiting all week to hear from Pat Cook to comment on a letter which we originally wanted to give to HfR on 14th. It turned out that she had misunderstood and thought she only had to answer if she thought there should be amendments. However, we sent a letter addressing the issues she had raised to Steve Clifford (church leader), Chris Williamson (HfR chairman), Linda Harding and Les and Liz Coveney (mentors). Chris Williamson phoned us that evening and invited us to a meeting with some of the International team; himself, Ralph Somerville and Liz and Les, to discuss practicalities, then following that, a meeting with Edwyn Pelly to discuss finance.

On Sunday 18th March, we talked as a family about finances for Romania. Rachel reminded us of the Ishmael song; *My God shall supply all my needs.* The song quotes Isaiah 58:11, so we looked it up.

> The Lord will guide you always;
> he will satisfy your needs in a sun-scorched land
> and will strengthen your frame.
> You will be like a well-watered garden,
> like a spring whose waters never fail.

Elaine noticed verse 12.

> Your people will rebuild the ancient ruins
> and will raise up the age-old foundations;
> you will be called Repairer of Broken Walls,
> Restorer of Streets with Dwellings.

Restorer of walls and of homes. It reminded her of a banner with that verse that had spoken to her at her Dad's 70th birthday service. She looked back in her diary, and she saw she had written about it and had asked God to show her how this related to a call to Romania. There were many instances like this which kept us secure in the fact that we were following the right path.

Ralph, Chris, Liz and Les met up with us on Friday 24th March. We felt a little intimidated at the start of the meeting, but Chris soon put our minds at ease by saying, "This is not a 'them and us' situation, we are all working together in this."

The meeting went very well, and we established that the sending was HfR serving us on the one hand and us serving HfR on the other. We also established that there were no major hurdles to get over save that of finance! There was a lot of money to raise to keep a family of five in Romania (Anne would be at University but with us for the long holidays)! From this meeting, a proposal was written to present to the main International team of the church the next week.

Following this, the International team and HfR endorsed us. The Oversight of the church gave us an amber light, verging on green depending on finance: God would have to do a miracle!

We spoke about the possibility of the move to our parents; we hadn't done so up to now because we wanted to be sure and not to put them through heartache unnecessarily. There was a mixed response from family and friends; some supported us in launching out on this adventure, others felt we were taking too great a risk with the girls' education. It was hard, especially when people close to us felt we were being reckless and irresponsible with our family, but there was a strong sense of affirmation from God over us which carried us through.

At some point around this time, it became obvious that we were not going to meet the September 2000 deadline, but it would have to be postponed a year to have everything in place. Elaine told her headteacher Angela Ewing that she would work full time until Christmas and then resign to get the family, house and everything ready for moving to Romania the next summer.

We were encouraged by Chris Williamson to start praying about a leader for a support group to pray for us. However, it proved a discouraging search as person after person said, "No" until there was no-one left amongst our circle of friends in church to ask. What was God saying?

There was one very significant meeting at this time. We met with Terry Reddin, the headteacher at Therfield, which Rachel and Becky now attended (and Abi would if we did not go to Romania) to talk things through. Unexpectedly he told us to grab the opportunity with both hands and that if we kept up with English and Maths, the education the girls would receive would be far and away richer than if they stayed at Therfield! He was extremely helpful and promised to help us in any way he could. There were three specific ways. First, guaranteeing places for Abi and Becky when we eventually returned from Romania. Second, textbooks and schemes of work to help Elaine teach the girls. Third, help and support for Rachel if she stayed to do her A levels. We agreed to meet again around Christmas to let him know of progress in our plans.

Elaine and I spent a week in Romania during August 2000; we had gone asking God for confirmation of our plans. Nothing negative came up apart from returning knowing we could not do this without finance. We met with Chris Williamson and put a challenge on the table; we needed 50% finance from church and HfR, and we would match it with 50% sponsorship from friends and family. Anne and Rachel had gone on another summer camp during this time too.

Earlier, we mentioned earlier that we had told God we were not going without the agreement of all our children. We had asked Anne to talk and pray with Abi and Rachel with Becky as they were so much younger. Anne of course, was fully up for it; she was now spending some of her gap year in Romania, split between three months in Brașov at a charity working with a baby orphanage in the centre of the city, and then six months after Christmas in Székelykeresztúr/Cristuru Secuiesc alongside

Laurie and Pippa Repath and Amy Sherwood, another gap year student from Pioneer People. Rachel had decided to remain in England with the Coleman family, close friends of ours until she had finished her A levels. Abi was happy to go if she could have a dog. Becky was much more cautious; she really didn't have peace. We told her that was fine and to carry on asking God what was right for her if it was right, God would give her peace.

One of the most significant principles that the girls still remark on to date is that we promised that if any of them didn't have total peace about moving out to Romania, then we wouldn't go. We felt it necessary for all girls to be with us in this adventure and not just to drag them along. They needed to have ownership of this vision too, and we found that this sustained our unity as a family in the most difficult of times in Romania. Our girls tell us now that this promise was both comforting and liberating at the same time.

It was a very frustrating Autumn, with many meetings about finance, lots of toing and froing, disagreements and then agreements etc. We still had not found anyone to lead our support cell. However, as usual, amid all this, God gave us a very significant time as a family when we went to visit Anne in her gap year in Brașov. We stayed in Casa Aurora, a missionary retreat centre, with its hosts Iosif and Ani Mich. This house and its hosts were another divine connection and were a lifeline for us many times whilst living in Romania.

We attended a church meeting with Anne, where the speaker said, "If you can't see where you're going with God, put one step forward and the light will go on for the next step. If you don't step forward, the light won't go on." This is something that we have quoted to ourselves and others *ad nauseum!* It helped us such a lot at the time and since. We all felt very much at home in the country again.

THE ROAD TO TRANSYLVANIA

CHAPTER 5

GOD IS A GOD OF MIRACLES

In December 2000, HfR and Pioneer People agreed to give us 25% each towards our living costs in Romania if we had our 50% promised by June 2001. We were also asked to attend the Management meetings of HfR to see the wider picture and keep in touch. Elaine wrote in her journal in January 2001,

> "There are three major hurdles to jump over; financial resources (slow to come in so far), someone to rent our house, and the right place to live out there."

Elaine also asked God to speak about the children's education. She wrote a deadline of 30th April. We had also heard that Laurie and Pippa would not be out there with us after all; they felt it right to return in the summer. On 10th April 2001, the next entry Elaine writes,

> "Things have changed drastically since last entry. Much encouragement and answers to prayer. Can't believe I haven't written it all down."

She then notes the encouragements and answers to prayer. In the financial realm, we had exceeded the target for the two years we would be out there due to some large cheques and some finance from totally unexpected sources. We had had a wonderful gift of a Scottish holiday at Easter.

Elaine had found Northstar UK, a virtual school online based at a Christian school in Manchester. They had suggested that we apply for September even if we didn't have the money as they would put our application into the hands of a charity to help pay fees for education.

Other parents from St. Andrew's school were initiating fundraising events for us in various forms. We needed help with computers, both technical support and hardware. Help arrived from the Clements family (who we knew in our past) who ran an IT business. Elaine had been on a prayer team led by Martin Scott to Székelykeresztúr/Cristuru Secuiesc to pray for the area. It was very encouraging, and she had gone to look at a house in Székelyudvarhely/Odorheiu Secuiesc with Chris Williamson. The location wasn't where we had expected to be, but it felt very right and was in the same valley. What we didn't know at the time was that as we would be working with many of the young people who had come out of the Children's Home - Székelyudvarhely/Odorheiu Secuiesc was a much more appropriate place to be.

The only hurdle that hadn't been overcome was someone to rent our house, and we needed that to pay the mortgage. Elaine did write that she was dealing with the grief that she was leaving her eldest two girls behind; that wasn't easy at all. On April 22nd Elaine wrote:

> *"An incredible answer to prayer, last week whilst I was away looking after an elderly aunt after an operation, a young couple in the church phoned and said to Phil that they were interested in renting. Today they*

came for lunch and said they liked it and would also like to use some of our furniture. We could store our remaining things in a top bedroom. They could move in on 1st Aug as we moved out to Romania. I had said to God that I wanted to rent out a home not a house. Natalie said to us it felt right because it felt like a home not a house that they were renting. So, our three hurdles are achieved before the deadline - God you are faithful to us"

Throughout this time, we attended cross-cultural training courses, including Kairos and Wycliffe Bible College to prepare ourselves; we also talked to like-minded people to prepare ourselves for what was to come.

Rachel was increasingly unsettled during April and May; she was unable to focus on her studying and wasn't sleeping. We discussed her previous decision to stay in England with her, and she said she wasn't at peace anymore. We encouraged her to pretend she was coming with us for a week and to see if she felt at peace with that frame of mind; she was a changed girl, we hadn't realised how much she had withdrawn into herself over it, and we had our bouncy, cheerful girl back again. So, Rachel was coming too. Again she had been trying to do *the right thing* educationally and trying to conform to society's expectations, but in the end God's provision prevailed and miraculously her time in Romania gave her more experience to prepare her for nursing training than she could ever have had in the UK.

Many people had asked us, "What is your project? Are you going to plant a church? What exactly will you do?" We had to answer that all we knew was that we had to go as *family*, to have a house which was a haven for the young people. We had no specific plan, but to be obedient to God's Call – the Slade family in Romania! It was to be a place where the young people could share in family life, to be involved with cooking, washing up, cleaning; all with a spiritual input. It was hard! The instinct to put a label to what we were doing to justify why we were going was strong, but we knew this wasn't what God wanted.

In every way God was asking us to buck the trend and do the unexpected, the unexplainable. Who would believe us that we were taking our family on an adventure into the unknown, living by faith, purely on the basis that we knew God had called us to serve HfR in Székelyudvarhely/Odorheiu Secuiesc? This was a lesson for life as it threw us back on God to show us the way forward, His way into the unexpected and the unexplainable. He was teaching us not to depend on man but on Him for all things.

The Bodrogi family (the family we had met the summer before) set to work locating various skilled people, and we had beds and furniture made. A new gas cooker and fridge were put in and secondhand table, chairs and seating etc. They were a godsend to us.

THE BODROGI FAMILY

Our home in Cobham was rented out to a number of different people as the Denkers moved out sooner than they had thought. The Bowleys, a South African Couple from Esher Green Baptist followed by a group of the youth from our church (some of whom had originally been in our Acorn group or Buzz) followed each other in renting our house.

CHAPTER 6

MOVING TO ROMANIA

Our moving date from Cobham was 1st August 2001. All four girls packed tightly into our minibus with essential clothes and personal items, and we left early in the morning to get the ferry to France.

As we set off on to the A3, the beginning of our adventure, unbelievably the minibus engine died. Yes, the engine cut out. We managed to get to the hard shoulder, but we couldn't believe it. However, as has happened so often in our lives, seeming catastrophes turn into an opportunity for God to work a miracle. Phil tried starting the engine again but nothing happened, so we prayed and reminded God that we were being obedient to Him against the odds and all human expectations. The family finished praying, Phil turned the key and it sprang back into life.

An exciting journey lay ahead travelling through France to Belgium and then through a small part of the Netherlands to Germany, then on to Austria, Hungary and finally Romania. Currency at that time was not as easy as it is now as we write this. We had French Francs, Belgium Francs, Dutch Guilders, Austrian Schillings, Hungarian Forints and Romania Lei to deal with. Borders were also long and tiring; getting into Hungary and Romania often took hours with long queues. The girls thought crossing from one county to another was great and we made it into a game. As we reached each country they would shout, "Culture Shock!" and wave their arms in the air. We stayed in various types of youth hostels on the way. Some were good purpose-built hostels; others were dormitory type rooms in schools. It was definitely an adventure, as you can see from the map on pages 208 and 209.

Arriving and setting up home in a different country and a foreign culture, even with some new friends that we had met can be a daunting task, especially as today, often means *today or tomorrow* and *yes* means *we would like to try to get it done, but it is not for sure, it depends what else happens*. We soon learnt the word, *bisztos* which is a Hungarian word meaning *for sure*. We started using this word when we needed things done within a time scale.

Towards the end of August, we returned to England for two weeks, staying in our own home, kindly invited by the Denker family. We finished tying up all the odds and ends to do with life in the UK and helped Anne pack for university. We then delivered her to Elaine's parents as they were to be her bolt hole whilst she was in the UK on her own; she went to Teacher Training College at Bishop Grossteste in Lincoln which was just half an hour away from them. It was extremely hard to go and leave her behind, tough for her and for us, especially as she had initiated the Romania dream, but she accepted the situation graciously.

We travelled back across Europe with the second lot of household goods to last us two years. The poor girls had been limited to one box of possessions each, including games and toys and one suitcase of clothes. They had left behind just one box each too as we couldn't take up any more room than one-bedroom space storing furniture and household goods in our house in Cobham. Throughout the six months that Elaine had spent at home, she had sorted and resorted our belongings until we had around 40% of our household goods and clothes left. Much of the stuff we gave away or sent to charity shops or dumped; it was amazing how releasing it felt to realise that people do indeed matter more than material possessions. It gave a tremendous sense of liberty to know that the only things that remained in your possession were the things that truly mattered the most; decluttering was definitely good for the soul!

Being fully aware of our promise to Abi that she could have a dog and knowing this was very much on our heart, we began to realise that finding a dog or puppy that was brought up in the English way was not easy. Dogs in Romania generally are kept as guard dogs.

On one of the first Saturdays we were there we decided to drive to Brașov, Poiana. Having visited Anne in Brașov while she was working with the Poplar's charity there, we had visited the Poiana mountain and knew it was beautiful with its cable lift. It's great in the winter for skiing and magnificent in the summer for gazing at amazing views across Romania.

We drove up the steep winding road to the ski lift and then boarded the cable car. On the way up, Abi pointed out a girl playing with a little puppy many metres below. Having agreed it made a lovely picture, we continued to the top, deciding that we would walk back down rather than taking the cable car.

Feeling extremely hot, hungry and tired by the time we got to the bottom, we decided it was time for a well-deserved meal. We picked a hotel restaurant that advertised its menu in

English. Halfway through the meal, the girls pointed outside to the same little girl with the same puppy who had been playing on the mountain. Having agreed they could go out and play whilst we finished our meal, we were surprised to see them communicating together really well. The girls then excitedly rushed in saying that the girl wanted to give them the puppy;

Abi had a beaming smile. We sorted out the bill and went out to meet the girl's parents who asked us in perfect English if we would like the puppy; it turned out that the family were from Israel on holiday and were returning the next day. The girl had found the puppy on the mountain and wanted to find a home for it. The parents, thinking that we were from Romania, asked how we spoke such good English. We began to explain why we were there; they explained that they too were involved in a charity project in their country managing a respite centre. The father suggested that this must be a God connection. We travelled back to our new home from Brașov with God's provision to Abi's prayer nestling into a garment on her lap. Our family now had a dog; Abi named him Barney.

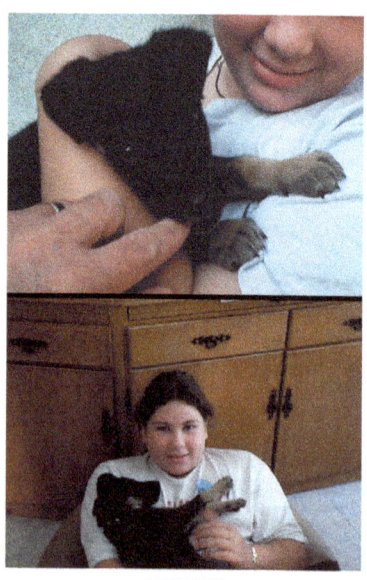

BARNEY

This reminder that God was interested in each minute detail of our lives inspired us to have faith for the bigger things of living there. Bodrogi Csaba took us to see the Manager of Rom Telecom, a member of the local Baptist church. He told him that we needed a reliable phone and internet system for the girl's home schooling. Willi, the manager explained that ISDN was coming, and he would initially only have ten lines, in the meantime our phone would be connected with the number of our choice!! We are not sure how much of a waiting list there was for the ISDN lines in Székelyudvarhely/Odorheiu Secuiesc, a large town with multiple businesses, but Willi gave us one of the ten lines and subject to power being available, we had a secure fast internet line for the girls. Praise God – another miracle!

Laurie and Pippa Repath had had the use of a German registered Peugeot car from a German charity working in Székelykeresztúr/Cristuru Secuiesc, and they had suggested that the charity allowed us to take it over until further notice. This they agreed to willingly. We now had an English registered minibus and a German registered Peugeot, the latter being a left-hand drive, perfect for Romania. The Bodrogi family helped us settle in. Kati, Csaba's wife, spent many hours showing Elaine and the girls how to cook Romanian recipes and how to bottle and preserve fruit and vegetables for the coming winter months. Csaba helped organise the utility services that we needed and contacts with local people in the community who could help us with everyday life. He also put us in contact with a local Consultant at the Székelyudvarhely/Odorheiu Secuiesc hospital, Lorinsz Csaba, someone who helped us enormously throughout our time there.

We always needed to have cash as nothing could be paid for by card. Food shopping was also very interesting; the best place to buy fruit and vegetables was the local market, and other goods could be acquired at tiny supermarkets called ABC which meant they sold everything, that is everything for a Romanian, not an English person as at that stage ready meals were unheard of and everything was cooked from fresh. There were frozen items, but from the look of them they had frozen several times after the frequent power cuts which occurred in the town.

In Székelykeresztúr/Cristuru Secuiesc, we were introduced to several couples who had connections with the German Charity Domus who were also working in the town. This included Martin and Dorit, a German couple; who introduced us, after six months, to a large cash and carry outlet on the outskirts of Brașov which revolutionised our shopping as we could buy in bulk at cost which in turn enabled us to provide a regular meal for many of the young people.

Bodrogi Csaba organised a daily delivery of bread from a baker in a local village who provided produce to many shops in the local town. We had a purpose-built bread box made and attached to the back of our big gates. Each morning around 5 am, a loaf of warm bread would arrive, what luxury! The girls set about decorating the house with Elaine; they enjoyed stencilling flowers and patterns onto the whitewashed walls to give the house a homelier feel.

CHAPTER 7

BAPTISM OF ICE

The first Autumn in Romania was not so much a baptism of fire but of ice! It snowed heavily at the beginning of November and then daily until mid-April, we didn't see a blade of grass in all that time. This was to be one of the worst winters in Romania for many years.

The temperature was usually around -15°C during the day and -30°C or lower at night. It was so cold that there were reports of guard dogs left out overnight freezing where they lay. We quickly got into a routine to cope with such temperatures. Our pipes were always frozen when we woke up, so the night before we filled

IN THE BACK GARDEN

huge pans with water and in the morning boiled it and poured it down the manhole cover outside to thaw the pipes into the house. If we had forgotten to do it or if the first couple of pans did not do the trick, we used snow and boiled it up and kept pouring hot water down until we had running water. This also affected the heating as the boiler used water directly from the mains to supply the leaking heating system. We dressed in several layers when we went out and made sure we had a scarf for our noses as anything in the nose would freeze if unprotected.

Romanian people always had lip balm in their pockets, both men and women, and would put in on their lips before entering the cold from anywhere. Both sexes would wear thermal underwear, even long-johns if necessary; something you would never see teenage boys wear in England! No bare skin or midriffs would be seen. People couldn't go out with wet hair. Our car and van's handbrakes were often frozen and sometimes the diesel.

We saw all sorts of sights on the road, such as lorry drivers using flame torches on the diesel tanks in their trucks to thaw the diesel. And yet, the buses and trains all ran on time; no-one used the snow as an excuse for lateness or an opportunity to miss school or work. The winters created great challenges to get anywhere; snow chains on the tyres were a necessity and so was winter diesel as fuel, even then on the coldest days the diesel froze, and we would be driving kangaroo style. Phil remembers one such occasion when he took Bodrogi Csaba and Kati to an evening Reception at Marosvásárhely/Targu Mures, and it took us twice as long as it should have done.

It was quite an education, but just living in these kinds of conditions as well as the culture shock, did make life tiring for the first year. We were also high up in the mountains at 476m which meant we had to get used to the thinner air, although it was very clean and pure. However, the warmth and hospitality of the people was something which will stay with us for the rest of our lives. Elaine writes in her journal,

> "Year one was great. Making relationships, opening our home, learning the language, getting used to the culture."

She said other things about year two which will be written later!

One of the major challenges on a regular basis was obtaining our visas. Romania was not in the EU at this time, and we had to apply every six months. This was often several days' work with the criteria changing each time; having to get more and more paperwork and papers stamped and re-stamped at different offices before going to the visa office which was in the main Police station in Csíkszereda/Miercurea Ciuc. It was an unpleasant experience, fighting our way to the front of the crowds of people also trying to be next to the little window in the wall, (queuing was not part of the Romanian culture), but Csaba was usually there with us. Each time was always a major challenge and having got the visas, it was an occasion to celebrate with a meal or a party. The final visa before we came home was given for two years. Why could they have not done that before? Probably because we needed to be there for three years before they could? Who knows!

To get anything in Romania it always took ages; we had to jump through so many hoops and red tape, but there was always such relief when it was achieved. Bodrogi Csaba always said that the pain of getting anything sorted increased the relief at the end and I guess it is why there always seemed to be a celebration of one sort or another going on. We began to find that keeping a diary to put in future events was purely academic; others found it a source of amusement.

Each day was never as we expected, and things always changed. People mattered in Romania, not things; priorities changed during the day depending on people's needs. If someone died in a village, it changed everything; all villagers would attend the funeral the following day to support the family. Employers expected this. Every day in the winter was a particular challenge; having managed to get water in the house, the next job was to dig the car out of the snow. A gypsy lad called Sandor (pronounced Shan-door) started coming to our home to seek regular work; the landlords had employed him in the past to do odd jobs. He was incredibly helpful in clearing the snow and doing other gardening jobs outside. In fact, it gave us the protection from others approaching us for work; because this was his territory and he made it known.

We soon found that privacy is very much an English concept. The, *my house is my castle* outlook did not prevail in Romania, it was more that your home was somewhere for all and sundry to come to. We were not expected to lock the door. The men or women reading the meters would expect to knock and come straight in. If you were inappropriately dressed, this did not seem a problem for them, that was life.

CHAPTER 8

SZÉKELYKERESCTÚR / CRISTURU SECUIESC

Much of our time in the beginning was spent in Székelykeresztúr/Cristuru Secuiesc. This is where the largest Children's Home in the Harghita region of Romania was situated; we say was, as it no longer exists, due to EU rules and regulations on joining the European Union.

The first and most significant language in this region was Hungarian, and so it was in this small town. Therefore, we took Hungarian lessons with a local Reform church priest called Gereb Laci; we had great fun learning the language with him, though we progressed at varying rates!

Phil began working very closely with the German foundation Domus. They had a programme of finding and managing flats for young people who had left the Children's Home or when they left full-time education. Some of these flats were in Székelykeresztur/Cristuru Secuiesc. There were others in Székelyudvarhely/Odorheiu Secuiesc and surrounding places.

The objective of this programme was to help the young people finishing their school education to live independently. Not an easy task as most had been institutionalised from an early age, and there was little interest from employers to take them on.

Often in Romania, a young person does not get paid for the first month as an employer sees this period as a probation period. You must do very well in that first month to be kept on and often, most of them did not pass the test. Employers often used it to get free labour, knowing too well that they were not going to keep them after the first month. This led to a downward spiral of a feeling of worthlessness and hopelessness.

There were many cases like this, and Phil worked with Istvan (Pisti) from Domus to try and find sympathetic employers. He remembers going with one lad to a bakery where they said they would employ him. However, when he arrived with the lad and the manager saw the dark skin colour, he said that he was not able to employ him explaining that if the public knew there was a gypsy boy working in the bakery, it would have an effect on trade. He did seem really sorry not to be able to take him and apologised. It was always very hard for the young people to cook, buy the right food and spend only what they could afford. It had always been done for them, and this is where we felt as a family we could help. Having a home where they could come to, helping prepare a meal and make mistakes without being shouted at was what we were to model.

SZÉKELYKERESZTÚR/CRISTURU SECUIESC

SZÉKELYKERESCTÚR / CRISTURU SECUIESC

FORMER CHILDREN'S HOME

SZÉKELYKERESZTÚR/CRISTURU SECUIESC

THE ROAD TO TRANSYLVANIA

CHAPTER 9

CONTINUED SUPPORT AND EDUCATION

Back in England, our support was very strong. We knew the church community, family and friends were praying for us. Chris Williamson had overall stewardship of the house making sure our tenants didn't wreck the place, but Kerry Stephens was keeping an eye on our home on a regular basis and we transferred our home address to hers, so all post etc. went to her. Joyce May, Elaine's mum kept the financial side of the Cobham property in order with an efficient system of income and the paying of bills.

Abi and Becky were now in lesson mode using the online programme with a virtual class of children across the globe. Most of the class were from similar situations, where their parents were serving in various missionary type roles. North Star, the Christian school in Manchester, had its own classes with the internet service as an add-on. Many of the teachers taught in the school and online. They were able to chat via the internet, listen to lessons and send their work for marking. Elaine supervised and taught the girls in our home; both had purpose-built desks in their large bedroom, which made it easier to separate school from the other things that were going on in the home. School was normally long mornings Monday to

Friday. Sometimes Rachel supervised them, but normally she was with Phil, either in the community, shopping or cooking.

Of course, learning Hungarian was vital to communicate. Our language lessons with Gereb Laci proved to be very beneficial, and our sessions were often very comical. He was and continues to be a very good friend of Csaba's playing five-a-side-football weekly in the town. Laci also had some English classes that he ran in the town, called Essential English. He was very keen to teach English people Hungarian and was excited that Elaine might be able to help him with the English courses. We attended his lessons at his home in (Patakfalva/Valeni) weekly, where his wife, Eva and two boys became good friends. This became part of the girls' school week.

Laci's sense of humour was closely related to our own, and often we would spend more time laughing than learning which made the lessons easier to take, especially for me. Phil would say 'I am no linguist, probably following in my Father's footsteps. He often would recap the words of his French teacher, suggesting he would rather teach the headmaster's parrot than me.' We remember a time when Laci mentioned the Hungarian word for etcetara is *sotábé* pronounced *Shot a Bee*. Phil immediately held a pretend gun in the air and kept saying, "Shot a Bee" until Laci realised what Phil was saying and spent the next five minutes curled up in laughter which made the girls laugh even more.

Hungarian, the first language of the people we were going to be working with was not easy to learn and was probably one of Phil's biggest challenges. Elaine and the girls got on well with Hungarian. For him, it was probably good that the majority of people knew a little English and many knew a good deal of English, so always tried speaking in English to practice. Being able to speak and read English is seen as a great benefit in understanding technology, medicine and the many other areas which need an understanding of English as a major international Language. Many people we got to know in the area, would be able to speak or understand Hungarian, Romanian, English, German, Russian, Italian and often French

THE ROAD TO TRANSYLVANIA

CHAPTER 10

SZÉKELYKERESZTÚR / ODORHEIU SECUIESC

The town has grown amazingly to now include large international supermarkets like Kaufland, very large restaurants, hotels and spa and several large petrol stations.

Domus had a Monday morning briefing each week in their offices in Székelykeresztúr/Cristuru Secuiesc. Phil made it a priority to be there if he could. It was good to feel part of a team. Although we had come as family and had a role of being family to the young people, it was important to get an overall picture of the help and support that the young people were already receiving and rather than putting new things in place, to work alongside and supplement the great work already being achieved. Fazakas Pisti and Ani his wife, Burus Endre and Dorit as well as Pali Bacsi, the then leader of Domus Romania and others attended these meetings.

There was much practical support for the young people in Székelykeresztúr/Cristuru Secuiesc, but many of the youth were moving to flats in Székelyudvarhely/Odorheiu Secuiesc as this was where there was more opportunity for work. Domus felt that as we were living there, it was like a base in the town and we were very pleased we felt we could work together with them there. Phil spent a lot of time with Pisti who travelled over most days to the town, and they would go and visit the young people together either in the flats which they were renting from Domus or at their workplace. We often took them to possible employers and encouraged them to find work and help deal with the problems they faced as employees with a children's home background. A Monday morning meeting now shifted to our home where Phil met with Pisti and Dorit after their earlier meeting in the Domus office in Székelykeresztúr/Cristuru Secuiesc.

We looked for a suitable church to attend; having tried the traditional Baptists in Udvarhely, we decided to look for a freer type of worship. Sometimes we drove to Székelykeresztúr/Cristuru Secuiesc to the Catholic church which we knew quite well; the Priest there was very involved with helping and supporting the Children's Home including arranging sponsorship from Italy for many of the children. A lot of the young people we knew attended, and it was good to be with them. As more and more moved to Székelyudvarhely/Odorheiu Secuiesc, we were invited to attend Szent Miklos, the big Catholic church in the centre of the town. At 6 pm on a Sunday, they held a Youth Mass; although every age seemed to attend, it was predominantly a youth congregation with a youth worship group and band. This started to become a regular feature of our Sundays. There was also a discipleship group that met during the week. They called it the Charismatic Catholic Group and were very open to the Holy Spirit's leading.

Rachel was with us for the first year until she decided she would do a Nursing Diploma at Anglia Ruskin University in Chelmsford near Elaine's sister's family. We returned to England for the summer holidays before she started in the September. We stayed in about eight different homes as friends invited us to be in their houses while they were away. We were very grateful for the hospitality and kindness of people, but this was not a restful time and proved to be a helpful lesson in the future about how we look after people who come home from abroad. It was even harder to leave not just Anne but Rachel as well in the UK. We returned to Romania with just Abi and Becky. Rachel had played an important part in our ministry in the previous year and was a great loss to us. She had been an immense support to me with language translation. During her year, she had had some medical experience as we were able to find a contact who was a district nurse who regularly took Rachel on her rounds with her.

In the second year, we felt it would be good to have a meeting in our house on a Sunday. This idea was one that evolved. Some asked if they could cook a meal beforehand and before we knew it, we were regularly feeding both physically and spiritually around sixty young people every other Sunday. They had to wash up too if they ate and little by little, we were able to help them with life-skills, important after having lived in an institution. God seemed to provide a miracle in these times; we did not have a lot of money for food, but whatever we bought seemed to be enough. At other times during the week, we would cook a meal for the four of us but by the time we sat down there would be ten, and we just added another cup of water in the soup and it always was enough.

After these times on a Sunday, we would go to the Catholic church for youth mass with the young people. The Priest that took the youth Mass came to speak to the young people about his Christian journey, how it had been during the Communist years and the Call of God in his life at that time. Julia and Berci were a couple who quickly became a large part of our Romanian journey and were part of the church group mentioned above. Julia was a lovely Christian filled with the Spirit who had been brought along by someone else to help on an Alpha camp for the young people during the second year. We prayed with her that she would find a godly partner and this she did on a train going to a conference in Marosvásárhely/Targu Mures. The first meeting seemed to be it! They were both overjoyed.

RACHEL WITH FRIENDS

ANNE WITH FRIENDS

FRIENDS BY OUR HOME

PHIL WITH CHILDREN AT SCHOOL

Sometimes at our Sunday times, we had German visitors from the German charity Domus or another German charity in Bautzen. Interestingly the young people began to call these times church, which of course it was, but it was not for us to give it that label. Normally we had to collect them; one or two journeys to Székelykeresztúr/Cristuru Secuiesc by minibus and one to Szentegyháza/Vlăhița where some of the young people were at boarding school. Often, we would set off in the snow not knowing if we would get there and back. Phil remembers one such journey, Elaine had taken some back to Székelykeresztúr/Cristuru Secuiesc in the car, others had gone on the train, and he took a group back to Szentegyháza/Vlăhița. The snow got heavier and heavier, and the young people just kept singing worship songs to a tape in the van. We continued to pray for safety. Phil was glad he had one of his own girls with him as he needed to put the snow chains on during the way back.

One very cold winter's night, Elaine went outside to lock the gate. The next thing we knew, she was banging at the window with blood all over her face. She had completely split open her lip up to her nose having run down to the gate because it was so cold and catapulted over a metal rod which a lad had left sticking out after some work he had done. We held it all together with a towel and made an emergency call to the consultant at the hospital who we mentioned in Chapter 1 and whom we had come to know very well. Phil explained what had happened and he said to bring Elaine immediately to the hospital, and he would meet us on the front steps. Lorinc Csaba was in his running gear and with one look at Elaine made a phone call. He explained that he was phoning the Face specialist who amazingly lived around the corner and he would be there in ten minutes. He was the only face surgeon for that region!

The specialist knew exactly what to do; without anaesthetic went to work to bring both parts of the upper lip together. Some healing had miraculously taken place to heal the split to the nose, but the lip was still split apart. He said not to worry, and she would be looking like Sophia Loren when it was finished. The girls had been praying and were quite scared. From what we had seen, it looked very bad. God worked many miracles that night. Elaine's lip healed perfectly because the surgeon got to work so quickly, and unless you look very carefully and knew what you were looking for you would not notice the scar.

THE ROAD TO TRANSYLVANIA

CHAPTER 11

MISSING HOME AND SOME ANSWERS

By the end of the first year, the lack of privacy exhausted us; anyone and everyone expected to be able to call at any time. We had difficulty finding family time together. The young people knew that they had to be quiet if they came whilst Elaine was teaching the girls, but it didn't make a lot of difference. If Phil wasn't there, Elaine was expected to deal with visitors even though she was busy with the girls.

We decided we needed to block out rest time. However, we were misunderstood. The people thought we had forgotten to open the front gate and visitors continued to call loudly or jump over the fence, then tell us we had forgotten to unlock the gate. We realised that to get any time to ourselves that we would need to go away; staying in our home to rest was not an option. We booked Casa Aurora once a month; the retreat centre we had stayed in when visiting Anne during her gap year. Iosif and Ani Mich were very welcoming and became good friends. The centre became a haven for us as a family; there was a kitchen, a games room, we were close to the city and to Poiana Brașov Mountain. Iosif was also available to drive people to and from Bucharest airport, and we used him on a regular basis to transport visitors or ourselves there and back.

Close friends and family came out to see and support us. The Coleman family (our children grew up with theirs) came to visit us during the Easter period in 2002; we had some adventures together whilst they were with us. We decided to take both the minibus and car to pick them up from Bucharest airport. The journey from our home to the airport took five to six hours and was uneventful. However, the return journey was not.

As we reached Sinaia in the Carpathian Mountains; a snow blizzard began, it got thicker and thicker. It developed into a full-blown snowstorm and was inches deep within minutes. As we were driving along one of the mountain roads, Phil realised that the car Elaine was driving was no longer behind me. In fact, there was no traffic. He then got a call from Elaine who said, "I've had an accident." No details but she was upset. Phil drove back along the road. Her car had slid across the icy road and scratched a Mercedes going the other way. The main thing was that no one was hurt; but the lady driver was very angry as she said she had no insurance and demanded that we pay up immediately. We refused, as in Romania any accident must be reported to the Police and no bodywork can be done to the car without a Police report.

It was cold, dark and we were all tired but even in this incident God took care of us all. We managed to ring Iosif at Casa Aurora in Brașov and told him what had happened; he said he would drive to Azuga Police station and we should meet him there in the next town. Iosif again was God's provision for us as he sorted things out at the Police station. He made sure we had the correct documents and that things had been sorted before we drove back in convoy to Brașov. Fortunately, the car was driveable. Iosif and Ani put us all up for the night and ordered a massive pizza. It was amazing that they had no guests at the time as there were eleven of us in total to stay. We had a great time with the Coleman family, and we went back to Brașov to climb Poiana mountain with them.

Whilst we were there, we began to understand the Romanian health and safety policies; what policies? Sometimes you might come across a massive hole in the road where repairs were being done with no warning notice apart from a sign on a stick somewhere nearby.

It was while we were in Brașov having a coffee in a café that an almighty crash came from the toilets. Knowing that Sarah and Fiona were in there, the girls went to investigate to find that Sarah had pulled the chain on the overhead cistern and it was now in pieces on the floor. The owner of the café, rather than apologise that the cistern had not been fixed to the wall securely, was very upset and expected us to pay for it; despite the fact that Sarah could have been killed if it had landed on her head. Praise God that she had not been hurt. We thought as a gesture that the café would not charge us for the drinks, but they insisted we paid and as we left, they were still insisting we paid for the repair. A different way of looking at things. If something happens it is your fault for touching it, using it or not being more careful. We soon learnt that the customer is always wrong. Had Sarah been injured, it may well have been a different story; if someone is in trouble or injured or has broken down in a car, everyone stops to help. I think this was one of the refreshing things we found in Romania as said before; people matter more than things.

As the Colemans went home, Elaine's parents came out to see us for two weeks. It was good to spend time with them and to show them what life was like for us. One memorable time was Elaine's Dad (he had become a Christian in the Army and then was later ordained as a minister) shared with around fifty young people about his background. The theme was - What starts bad doesn't have to end bad. His story was probably very similar to some of the young people there. The talk had a profound effect on some. This is what he said:

"I understand that each of you have experienced difficult and hard times as you have grown up. So, let me share with you a little about my own life, which I trust will encourage you to understand that you do not have to end and continue in life as you began.

As you trust God you will know better days ahead. Both of my parents were born of single mothers in what we call the Workhouse, that is a place for very poor people - a bit like your Orphanages. When they grew up, they married each other and had four sons. I was the third to be born. We had a small dirty home living in one room. We all, six of us, slept in the same bed, sharing the nasty biting bugs and the fleas on our bodies and in our hair. We had no shoes on our feet and rags were our clothing day and night.

When I was five and my youngest brother a small baby my parents were prosecuted, that is taken to Court and charged with the wilful neglect of their children. They were sent to Prison. Our family was split up and never came together again. I went from one home to another many times throughout my boyhood. Some were good and some were bad. I did not know the love of father and mother. However, some kind people, like Phil and Elaine to you, took an interest in me. They showed me that I did not have to grow up as I began, and I want to tell you that God has been very good to me from those early difficult days.

I want to encourage you to trust God, take advantage of people who want to help you, and you will be able to encourage other YP young people as you grow up."

The Maxwell family came out to us in October 2003. They got to know many of the young people there, and it was a bonus for Abi and Becky to show their cousins around. The Maxwells wrote:

"We particularly remember the wonderful sense of community that was tangible at the Slade home. At mealtimes, if someone turned up at the door, another place was simply laid, and they were squeezed in around the table. The food always seemed to stretch! Laughter and eager conversation characterised the atmosphere. There never seemed to be a time when someone wasn't popping in for one reason or another. The poverty of some was particularly striking. As in so many countries yet to be overtaken by materialism, their openness and generosity was humbling. Nic particularly remembers a visit to a Special School where the equipment was sparse in comparison to the UK, but the pupils were obviously happy and well loved. Every day we seemed to be amazed by something new. It really was a holiday with a difference!"

Linda Harding (who writes in the forward) and Miki from Japan visited us, so did a prayer team consisting of Jenny Moore, Val Bruce and Ralph and Ruth Somerville. Both visits recharged us spiritually as they stood with us on the front line of ministry. Members of HfR regularly came to see us too to check we were coping and to talk through our ministry. It was quite lonely living in Székelyudvarhely/Odorheiu Secuiesc as the only English family. Sometimes it was exhausting to constantly be in another culture with another language despite the friends and nuclear family closeness that we enjoyed. We just needed some normality, and this was helped by the visits from the UK and regular letters. Helen Goddard was the best at letter writing. She sent monthly letters chatting about normal everyday events at home. This helped us feel more in touch with our culture, and we eagerly anticipated those letters in the post box on the gate. Each morning the girls would run to the box and check and if there was such a letter, we would stop everything and read it together; we felt so supported and loved by such a letter.

Another lifeline was our great friend S-P O'Mahony, also from Pioneer People in Cobham, who had become an Irish diplomat for Hungary and Romania and was based in Budapest. His move there in 1999 and subsequently to Transylvania in 2009, was inspired during his time as the Chairman of Heart for Romania between 1996-99. He helped and advised us in many areas. He was involved with Opportunity Microcredit Romania (OMRO) since 2005 as a Board Member and then as CEO until 2016. Since 2013, S-P has served on the Board of The Royal Foundation of Margareta of Romania, which has been serving the excluded & disadvantaged there for more than thirty years. He now lives in Cluj, the unofficial capital of Transylvania, with his young family. S-P was one of God's provisions for us.

He invited us to Budapest on a few occasions during the time we lived in Romania. We left on a train from Sighisoara going directly to Budapest. As we got to the Hungarian border and the train stopped, and Romanian border police checked and stamped our passports and tickets, speaking in Romanian. We then slowly moved for a few minutes and stopped again, and this time we were asked by Hungarian Border Police for the same documents.

It was fun being met by S-P with a blue diplomat plated car. We seemed to zoom through the city and found ourselves at a very interesting apartment to stay in. The rooms were all on one floor, with one room leading into the next in a very large old terraced home. The rooms were filled with musical instruments and antique furniture and had the feel of a home of a composer such as Franz Liszt. Who had lived here and why was all this stuff still here? Had they moved out so that we could have the apartment as they needed money? Nobody seemed to know. We think S-P was quite bemused about the property he had rented for us, having not seen it until we all arrived but was relying on friends to find a place for us. The girls found it exciting and bizarre all at the same time, discovering nooks and crannies. We have never used an antique toilet before, and this was one, in a small, slightly smelly bathroom.

Discovering Budapest and trying to understand the transport system was a great time for us. We even found Cadburys chocolate, although disappointingly it never seemed to taste the same as the Cadburys bought in England.

The Children's Railway (Gyermekvasút) in the Buda hills was a hit with all the family. It was built after World War II and was originally called Pioneer's railway, something the girls picked up on straight away. The railway is still run by children under the supervision of adult railway workers. There are various jobs for children, from selling tickets to traffic management. Of course, the girls wanted to know how the children could do this and not be at school. A little research told us that the railway is run by young people aged between 10 and 15. Each child joins a group for a 15-day period. They are all volunteers and continue their schooling on site.

What would our next trip to Budapest be like? We arrived to find we were to have breakfast at one of the best hotels overlooking the Danube. No, it was not going to be breakfast, but a Champagne Brunch. S-P met us, and we walked along the banks of the Danube to the hotel and into the dining area. The girls' eyes were bulging as we saw the different displays of food and drink, including of course, champagne.

On our third visit we stayed at S-P's apartment. They were away for a few days, so we had it to ourselves. They probably felt it would provide no surprises after our other property adventures. It had amazing views from the Buda side of Budapest across the Danube to the Pest area.

In the first Autumn 2001, S-P invited me to a business conference with the theme of Christian ethics in business; Elaine came with me and I also took Bodrogi Csaba with me to Marosvásárhely/Targu Mures. Csaba was at this time working as a senior tax officer in the local authority; the conference seemed to have a life-changing influence on Csaba. Firstly, he saw Romanian and Hungarian people working together and having fellowship together, something he had never experienced. Secondly, Phil believes his whole outlook on life and on his work made a dramatic shift. As you will see from his article later, it changed his life forever.

CHAPTER 12

CHILDREN'S HOME CLOSING

The Orphanage in Székelykeresztúr/Cristuru Secuiesc was closed in Autumn 2002 - due to a wider policy to close all such homes as a condition of entry into the EU. Those who were still in fulltime education were relocated to flats in various locations across the county with a team of educators looking after them on an eight-hour rota basis.

It was also at this time that Richard and Emily Bailey were looking to set up one such home where a family group could be housed with house parents. There was already a German model which had been running for some time which was successful. Before this could be achieved, it was important to establish a charitable Romanian Foundation. Phil was given the task of investigating how to set it up and with the help of Bernád Rozi and Bodrogi Csaba, we looked for a suitable lawyer who could help work on this for HfR. A lawyer was chosen from Székelyudvarhely/Odorheiu Secuiesc, and the process demanded lots of paperwork, meetings and time. David Taylor came to Romania to sign papers as he was to be the Founder of the organisation. Drawing up the Constitution was a difficult and expensive process as everything had to be translated by an official translator. Eventually the Foundation was established, and a house acquired in Fiatfalva. Suitable house parents were found, and Richard and Emily went about setting up the home. They lived in Székelykeresztúr/Cristuru Secuiesc for six months, and Richard became Chairman of the Foundation called Fundatia Heart for Romania.

Another memorable graduation ceremony was that of Sztoika Csaba and Bartor Sandor in Székelyudvarhely/Odorheiu Secuiesc just before we came back to England. Csaba having no suit to wear was dressed up in my father's Chester Barry suit, which had originated from Austin Reed's in Regent Street where my Dad had worked. Sztoika was probably the best dressed man in Székelyudvarhely/Odorheiu Secuiesc that day. Celebrating these occasions with them were very important as we stood in as family for them. Before the children's home was closed, we were invited to the last of the school graduation ceremonies locally when many of the young people left their state education. Many of them were now to go to the state-run apartments around the district.

Visiting these homes now became part of our regular activity because many of them were in other towns and the young people, who had all been together in the children's home, felt isolated. These homes were in Székelykeresztúr/Cristuru Secuiesc, Székelyudvarhely/Odorheiu Secuiesc, Vlăhița and Csíkszereda. We also visited some who had gone to schools further afield such as Gyergyószentmiklós/Gheorgheni; this included girls who were in further education. We would take gifts, trying to remember the various birthdays, and often took them out for a meal. These were times that the young people looked forward to. We would regularly sing together and pray into the various needs.

CHAPTER 13

PHIL'S FATHER AND FAMILY

One of the sad things that happened whilst we were in Romania was that Phil's Father died. We knew that he was not well. When Elaine went home for some medical tests, she advised Phil to return to see him as quickly as possible. He travelled back to the UK on the same plane which had brought Elaine back to Romania after the tests. Dad was very happy that we were in Romania doing what God wanted us to do, but it was hard knowing that he was probably close to the end of his life.

Phil's Father was now aged 92; he had grown up in Dorset in Gillingham, where his parents had owned a men's outfitters called, Slade Men's Outfitters. The place where the shop was, has now been developed as the Slade Centre. He served during the war in the medical corps, spending much time in Burma. He also had risked his life protecting the water reservoirs at Walton on Thames. He recalled the time when they were sheltering from a bombing frenzy when the building that they were in collapsed and water started flooding it. He was the only one to survive that day. His near misses seemed to be a regular occurrence. He also recalls when he was a young man riding a motorbike, he came off at a crossroads called Canards Grave in

Somerset. Having regained consciousness, he recalled a man saying, "be 'e dead?"

Phil writes, "I think I gained my sense of humour from my Dad. He was always up to practical jokes and loved telling stories. I admired my Father and especially that he was a man of God who loved showing me life skills, carpentry, bike repair, making up the fire. He took me with him to Austin Reeds in Regent Street in London when I was 15 one Saturday. I learned how to speak with customers in a very diplomatic way, help them put on a jacket and became skilled at good PR. This became a regular Saturday adventure, and sometimes when the weather was good, I would cycle with him each way. It was nine miles from Leytonstone to Regents Street. It was then that I realised that when an American Gentleman asked to see some 'pants' he meant trousers. A little embarrassing for a young lad who had no idea of differences between languages.

He met my Mum at a Christian conference centre in the Lake District at an event called the Keswick Convention. They married and moved to Hackney in East London, where I was born. We moved to my Mother's family in Birkenhead for a year before moving to a more settled home in Leytonstone. I don't remember much about the first few years but have lovely memories of our time in Leytonstone.

We attended a church called St Luke's in Hackney where my Father was a churchwarden and Scout leader. I often cycled to church with my Dad whilst Mum went on the bus; I also cycled over on a Sunday afternoon to have organ lessons with a very lively organ player called Allen Goh. Sadly, my Mother died when I was 15. She had taught me many domestic skills, including cooking and gardening; her standard geraniums were a talking point for all passers-by. I must have got a love of horticulture from her as she taught me what a weed was and what was not a weed. I later had my own allotment at the age of 16 and then went into an apprenticeship in horticulture with the former Greater London Council.

It was while I was an apprentice based in Victoria Park in Hackney that I began to feel that the eldest daughter of the vicar was very attractive. I had known her and her sister when my Mum was alive. Mum used to have them over on a Saturday sometimes, and we were friends. Elaine eventually became more than a friend despite our six-year age gap, and we were married as she started her third year of university at Goldsmith's in South London.

My Father had remarried by this time to Janet Cockett. Although the first few years were not plain sailing for them, they looked after each other well. Dad came to his resting place knowing that Janet cared very deeply for him. I was not at his side when he died, but it brought some relief knowing that Rachel had been with him just before he passed away. They shared a joke and some laughter."

THE ROAD TO TRANSYLVANIA

CHAPTER 14

DRINKING WATER AND FOOD

We as a family took various trips around the region that we lived in. During one trip to Segesvár/Sighisoara, we discovered a place in the fortified area at the top of the town called, House On The Rock. We went inside to find a coffee shop and various rooms including, an internet type café area. Noting the number of English banners around the place, we asked a little more. It was a Christian Foundation, set up by the husband of the lady we were talking to. She explained that before moving to the USA where they had set up the foundation, they had lived in Esher! She also took us up to a lending book library where with great delight we found the books were 50% English and 50% Romanian. Our girls, who had not been able to bring many books with them, set about busily choosing books to borrow. This then became a regular visit to exchange books. We also found a local shop which sold guitars cheaply, so we were able to buy a couple for the young people Elaine was teaching how to play.

A trip to Sighisoara also normally meant a good meal. We had found an excellent Pizza place and an excellent Restaurant called Joker. This was always a treat and very cheap compared to UK prices at that time.

We rented our home in Udvarhely from a Unitarian Priest and his wife, who lived about an hour away in a village called Székelyderzs/Dârjiu. Dénes was the priest of a very ancient church there and his wife Piroska owned a cheese-making business, supplying cheese to local shops in the town and beyond. We had once made a trip there with horse and cart with the Bodrogi family driven by Bitszi, the owner of the horse and cart. The journey was one of the most memorable we can remember apart from the physical toll of the bumping and grinding of the cart, as we sang a mixture of English and Hungarian songs all the way and the way back. It was a very hot day, we had ice creams and our return journey was mostly in the dark. We had very sore backsides the next day.

The experiences that we had with the Bodrogi family could fill the pages of this book. We had barbecues by rivers in the middle of nowhere, and picnics in the most unusual places. Hungarian/Romanian people loved the outdoor life and would eat outside in the summer whenever and wherever they could.

Pig killings were an annual event when friends and family come together. People would buy the pig and bring it home by horse and cart, then to make a fire, kill the pig and singe the hairs off by rolling it around in a straw fire. On one of these occasions, Paul Knowlson and Jodie Papworth who were living with us at the time, were asked to eat a piece of the ear and tail, a delicacy, especially assigned for visitors.

Pig killings are done in the winter months and often in temperatures which are well below freezing, so a good deal of Palinka (known as fire water – basically a plum liquor) is consumed at the same time to keep warm! The preparation of the meat was all done in an outhouse where specialties such as brain soup were cooked. The intestines were cleaned out to provide skins for sausages, and a manual mincer was used for making the various sausages seasoned with various herbs and spices. The kitchen area was a hive of industry; Paul (who writes later in the book) rolled up his sleeves and surprised the women as he did a major job of washing up, a job only done by women. Elaine built up her muscles as she turned the mincer handle for hours, and the girls were taught how to use the sausage machine. Phil helped cut up meat and prepare it. This was an amazing community festival, which was then repeated at a neighbour's house the following week until the entire neighbourhood had their pig meat for the winter months.

Another major challenge of living in Romania was finding drinking water. Tap water is only good for washing, and all other water needs to be acquired or purchased. The main source of drinking water came from springs; of which there are a number around the area. Many of them did however carry a strong taste of iron or minerals. Some were known to be of great health benefits, but collecting the water was a weekly chore and took time.

Our main source of water was from a spring called Erzsebet Kut – a spring that had been used for the summer camps, situated at the foot of the field where tents and a campsite had been regularly set up each summer. This is where Anne had first fallen in love with Romania in 1996 when she was 14, and then where Phil had made many friends whilst on camp with Anne in 1998.

The water from the spring was very clear and delicious. We needed to fill plastic bottles, so we took crates of two-litre bottles which we filled up each time. It could take two or three of us a couple of hours, especially during the third year when the stream was sluggish due to drought. Cooking for so many young people meant frequent visits to the stream, although they did help us fill the bottles. Most of these springs still exist today, and you will see cars parked alongside them with people filling up empty water bottles.

CHAPTER 15

THIRD YEAR

Having originally gone to Romania for two years, it became clear that we should stay for a further twelve months. Funding had only been agreed for the initial period, and the church was no longer in a position to help us. However, HfR and the individuals who had sponsored us faithfully would continue to do so and supported our vision.

Our holiday in England over Easter after my Dad's funeral included a financial supporting drive, making it possible to stay for a third year through family and friends' generosity. Money was often on my mind during those three years as it seemed like we were spending more than our sponsorship income. Heating was expensive, so were vehicles and food for so many (we often had young people living with us for short times) and travelling back and forth to the UK. Phil kept a strict account record, but miraculously there always seemed to be more money in the account than there was on paper. God was faithful; we always seemed to have enough and often enough to bless others as well.

In the summer as we began our third year, we felt we needed a holiday in Romania. We were given details of an apartment in a minister's home close to Constanta on the Black sea. Anne and Rachel had joined us for the summer. We were so looking forward to the rest. Having arrived at the home it became clear that the apartment was in fact, three bedrooms in their home and shared facilities for cooking and bathing. It wasn't what we had in mind; in fact, we had to go through their bedroom to get to the bathroom at night. It was all on one floor. We decided we needed to stay out for most of the day.

One trip was to a beach where people had driven across the dunes, so we parked close to the beach. We had a lovely day but driving off the dunes, the minibus got firmly stuck. The more I tried to get free, the deeper the wheels sunk into the sand. There was a group close by with a four-wheel drive that saw our predicament. It turned out they were Christians connected to Moldova. Despite all this, the beach was amazing, and the sand and sea were hot.

AT THE BEACH

We spent time talking as they rescued our vehicle from the pit! They mentioned that the Doulos ship run by Operation Mobilisation (OM) was at the docks in Constanta and that we should visit. We had known of the ship as it had been moored in London some years before. It was a mission ship bringing educational and spiritual books to different parts of the world. It was basically a floating bookshop. The large team on board all had their various areas of work on the ship but also other ministries which were used at the port where they docked, often supporting existing local ministries.

The next day, we were given a tour and Anne, who was now completing her teaching degree, was very interested in the educational part for the ship. They had a school on board for the children of families serving on board. Anne spent time with one of the teachers who told her that they might have a vacancy in a year or two as one of the teachers would be leaving. We could see Anne becoming more and more interested. The teacher invited us back as special guests to the morning service and for lunch the next day. This was for invited guests only and the crew. It was great to participate in an English service and to speak with so many Christians in English.

VISITING THE DOULOS SHIP

God works in mysterious ways; ways we could not even begin to plan out. From a minibus stuck in the sand to God's calling on Anne's life as she went to serve as a teacher on the ship having completed her first year of teaching. That's not all; Anne met Izwe, a South African who arrived on the ship at the same time as her. He worked as an engineer in the boiler room. He had been a youth pastor and preacher in a South African church and had been called to serve on the Doulos as well for two years. Anne and Izwe were married after they had served on the ship and we now have two grandchildren. Zoë and Phoebe. I guess the message is, don't worry if you get stuck... God has a plan.

Another day on our holiday we decided to meet up with Pisti and Ani's family (in Domus from Székelykeresztúr/Cristuru Secuiesc) and their friends. We had found out that they would be at the Black Sea at the same time as us. It took some time to find them on the beach as we had been told to meet them by the, "Ballon." Pisti had said you couldn't miss it; it's on the beach up high. We were looking for something which said Ballon, finally we realised that he meant a very large balloon. He just couldn't understand how we hadn't seen it. We had a lovely day together, finishing with a dance party on the beach until late. Pisti did a great rendition of, I Shot the Sheriff by Bob Marley. This was to seal our friendship for the future with the Fazakas family. Ani got on very well with Elaine as it was one of those relationships in which they felt they had always known each other; a bit like Elaine's relationship with Bodrogi Kati.

We felt we needed an additional pair of hands in the third year. Jodie Papworth, whose father was very much involved in HfR and camps, had recently returned to the UK after spending her gap year with us. Paul Knowlson, a friend from church offered to come and live with us Phil enjoyed having another man about the house. Paul helped him a lot with the young people and later with Abi's schooling when Elaine returned to England while Becky sat her GCSEs.

CHAPTER 16

SUPPORTING THE YOUNG PEOPLE

As we mentioned earlier on, we believed we were to be like Mum and Dad to the young people who had left the children's home. This meant helping them with decisions, finding work and finding flats for them to live in.

Two years earlier, Gazsi had left the children's home and had been out of work ever since. That doesn't mean he hadn't tried other employment. The problem with many of his employers was that they would take him on for a trial month without pay and then say goodbye to him once the month was up. It had left him feeling totally rejected. Many of the young people had little discipline or understanding of work ethics as they hadn't lived in a family environment.

Gazsi was one such lad who had basically given up. A neighbour who was a member of the local Baptist church with a vehicle body repair garage agreed to take him on. We paid Gazsi for the first three months while he learnt to get to work on time, and to learn to take responsibilities such as calling in sick where necessary. He came to have lunch with us on most days, and we chatted through the progress that was taking place. His whole demeanour started to change as an element of self-worth started to grow. Having agreed with his employer that he was improving his skills at the work, we agreed to pay another three months at half pay while the employer would pay the other half. Before the further three months was up, his employer told us he was going to pay his full wages and officially signed him up as an employee. We understand that he is managing his own building business in Hungary and is doing very well for himself.

It would not be correct to give the impression that everyone was a success story; some tried several times to be employable but did not succeed. There were those that wanted to go to university; some sponsored through Domus, others asked us to find help. There were several young people who were sponsored from the UK. Many of these were successful and are in England now. We made regular visits to Kolozsvár/Cluj-Napoca and Nagyvárad/Oradea where they were studying.

Paul Knowlson, who we mentioned earlier, helped with the girls schooling and around the home. We continued to see God's hand each day. Our home continued an open place where the young people came and often stayed. For one lad who had a drinking problem, it was often a place where he would come to sort himself out. He had found his parents and was devastated to find that their reaction to him was, "We didn't want you then, what makes you think we want you now?" It was heart-breaking for him and for us to witness.

We managed to find him a job with a sympathetic boss who knew he might have periods of absence after drinking but would start him afresh each time. We often felt that we were getting nowhere with him. Paul spent a lot of time helping him too. On reflection, we were surrogate parents by just being there. Praying and not judging; we learned anew to love with unconditional love. Not easy when you are trying to help and seeing little or no headway. We did get so frustrated at times. So easy to judge and still harder to keep forgiving. This is what God does with us all the time, and it taught us unequivocally about His passionate love for us.

Another young adult that we were fully involved with was Erika. She was expecting a baby and needing a place to live. Csaba helped us in finding a two-room flat for her and her baby. The father too was often on the scene but did very little to help as he was normally not working. Sponsorship helped this family with payment of the rent and food. Erika would also come and clean for us and help prepare food. This gave her some money for essentials and helped us too. Anne and Becky became her little girl's godparents.

Lidi wanted to get experience working with children, and we were able to get her an au pair position to start her off in the UK where she is currently still living. Many others were encouraged and sponsored through HfR; especially through Tim Poole who, upon retiring from teaching, spent a great deal of time in Romania.

Looking back at the time that Anne had on the Doulos; if Tim had not asked her to help with the summer camps he had organised, this story would have been different. As one looks back, you see small pieces of a large puzzle beginning to come together. It is a puzzle which involves lives, interwoven, making the whole. Our other daughters themselves were greatly impacted by the life-changing experience of living in Romania. All three have mission on their hearts, with Becky and Rachel serving abroad in their various ways and Abi on the mission's team of her church supporting missionaries from the home base.

THE ROAD TO TRANSYLVANIA

CHAPTER 17

END OF THE THIRD YEAR

Our three years were now coming to a close, and there seemed to be more planning needed for our return to the UK than there was for leaving. Sometimes it is easier to start something than to finish!

A year before in the Easter of 2003, we had organised an Alpha Conference hosted by the Hungarian co-ordinators from Budapest who had been introduced to us by S-P. Many of the church leaders from Székelyudvarhely/Odorheiu Secuiesc had come, including the Catholic church, the Reform church and the Baptist church. They wanted us to steer the events as the, "English knew how to do things." We did not attend ourselves, as we did not feel this was an English thing and knew it needed to be indigenous people taking ownership of Alpha within their community. So often we were asked our opinions because we were English and we had to learn to deflect the decisions and answers back to the Hungarian people as they, not we, were culturally relevant. There was very little feedback, and we did not pursue it as we felt we had facilitated the meeting and if it was right, it would go forward.

About one year later, we had a visitor from the Catholic

church who we knew. He invited us to a meeting to discuss Alpha in his home. We reiterated that we would not be involved in Alpha, but we would come. We arrived a few minutes before the meeting was due to start. He and his wife showed us into a room where we found a massive table. They were prepared for lots of people. As each person arrived, we were introduced to leaders from all the different churches, and our host explained that they had been meeting at 7 am on a Sunday morning to pray since the Alpha conference that we had facilitated the year before, and now they were ready to begin a course. It was an exciting time, and it showed us that if God prompts, obey. But then don't strive over making sure things happen: God just needs our willingness to set it in motion, and then He will do the rest.

In that third year, we could see that the churches were working more together. The girls often went to a midweek club run by the Baptist church called Készimunka or *Handiwork in English*; here they learned different crafts in the local culture. The main leader of this was a lady manager in Coates, a major cotton thread factory in the town. This contact helped with the employment of a couple of young people. We continued our good relationship with Laci and Eva. As well as teaching us Hungarian, he was the Reform church priest in a local village.

We also continued to go to youth mass with the young people and often went to a midweek group organised by a charismatic group from the catholic church; some of the youth came with us. Julia and Berci became the leaders of this group. They organised a weekend away in Marosvásárhely/Targu Mures for the young people, and many went. During the third year, I spent a lot of time with Szaba Istvan, a Reform church Priest working with an international Christian organisation in Targu Mures. He employed Grancsa Fulop for six months as a volunteer.

END OF THE THIRD YEAR

Fulop and Balazs Csaba both wanted to get to university. As they had missed out on getting the best from their schooling, a tutor was needed to get them to a level to pass the entry exam. Bodrogi Csaba found us a professor in Csíkszereda/Miercurea Ciuc who gave them private lessons on a Saturday. They were both successful and got into a Reform church university in Oradea where the president was Tőkés László. Partium Christian University was the first independent private Hungarian-language institution of higher education in Romania, accredited by the state. Tőkés László had been very much at the forefront of religious freedom during the communist years and a bishop of the Reform church. On my frequent visits to Oradea to meet up with Fulop and Balazs Csaba, Csaba would have much delight in inviting me to meet his friend, Tőkés László.

We also raised sponsorship for other young people through university. Judith and Sztoika Csaba went successfully through Cluj-Napoca/Kolozsvár University, and we are still very involved in their lives to this day.

With our final winter, we were beginning to long for an English season. Three to five months of below-freezing temperatures, daily snowfalls and ice takes its toll. You just cannot get so much done. Just living was hard work. Fresh snowfall was always good news for the gypsy lad who had attached himself to us for jobs. Snow meant money for him in clearing the snow from our drive and slope up to our gates. The slope always meant a driving challenge in the winter. Having to take a run at it and stopping in time not to ground the vehicle at the top.

We now faced the question of who would carry on supporting the youth in Romania when we were gone? God's plans are always the best and He had it sorted as always. We referred to

Julia and Berci in Chapter 10. They were the indigenous couple who were our answer to prayer regarding future continuation of God's work among the young people. They had become great friends of ours, and we were privileged to be at their wedding ceremony in the summer of 2004. The marriage was going to be after we returned to Cobham, so they brought forward the official wedding part at the local Town Hall. We were to be honoured guests, and we witnessed the official wedding. Julia and Berci continued our work with the young people after we moved back to England and they moved into our home as we were leaving. For them, this was an amazing provision and also for us. They now have three gorgeous daughters, but then we are biased!

JULIA, BERCI AND GIRLS

We mentioned that Martin and Dorit were people we also worked closely with. We formed a great friendship and spent an evening together each month with a meal and fellowship. Dorit helped Abi with her German schoolwork, and we would often pray together. Their English was definitely better than our German.

Sadly, after we left Romania they too had to go back to Germany; Dorit had a brain haemorrhage which partially paralysed her with a loss of memory from which she has now made some recovery. Martin was involved in a horrific motoring accident on his way back from Romania for which he needed many operations on his badly damaged arm. He has now fully recovered. Phil visited them in Germany on several occasions. Dorit has required a great deal of therapy and is involved with a local church in their Alpha course in Leipzig.

We started packing up. Three years' worth of *stuff* for a family now needed to be sorted once again. Elaine and Becky returned to England at the end of April for Becky to take her GCSE's up in Manchester at the school which had facilitated the online learning. It was daunting for them both having lived outside the UK culture for three years and feeling very out of touch with current life there. They had a much-appreciated bolt hole at Ruth and Ralph Somerville's in Cobham which became their base for the two months when they weren't up North sitting the exams. The *they* in the sentence before is used because Elaine and Becky faced this hurdle together and Elaine was able to support Becky through what could have been a traumatic ordeal. As always, we saw miracles of provision including a car, which kept our spirits securely grounded in God. Much of the furniture we had bought remained for Julia and Berci.

In July 2004, Abi and Phil returned with a packed minibus taking the familiar route via Budapest. Before the border, we stopped in a B&B where we had got to know the owners of a large house with a big garden and outside stone-built barbecue where they provided stoned-baked pizza. We always enjoyed staying there before facing the border. As usually there was a delay, and we waited to discover what they would require from us to get us through. We travelled across Europe staying at Youth Hostels in Austria, Germany and Belgium, before taking the ferry. Things have changed so much now at the borders; there are no queues and you often go through without stopping. We took a short holiday together in the UK after the GCSEs were finished and then returned to Romania to tie up all the ends, eventually moving back to the UK at the end of August.

We were very apprehensive about coming back to no job and a church which had decided to cease whilst we were away (Pioneer People). Good friends like our neighbours Liz & Les who lived opposite, were moving away to Wales as well. Our home in Cobham had been occupied by four groups of people during the three years. The last group were some older teenagers from our church. It was probably as well that we had no idea how the house was being used. Part of our front room had been turned into a ballpark, and it seemed many of the kids from the estate had enjoyed much fun there. Louis and many of the others were out and out evangelists, and a lot of good was done on the estate. Every part of our home seemed to house a person, including the outhouse and under the stairs. Since we have lived back in Cobham, we often bump into a young lad that tell us they had lived at our house. We think our neighbours were glad when we were back. We heard that our ground floor extension roof had been used as a music centre with drums and loudspeakers. Oh dear! A lot of damage limitation to be done. However, they were great and did a good job for the kids in the community.

Phil remembers going to Sainsbury's after we had returned to do some shopping. He recalls the sick feeling he had in his stomach seeing people filling their shopping trollies and so much variety of food available. Phil came back from the shops with nothing; he just could not face shopping.

However, we knew God's encouragement through the provision that came both financially and practically through the love of friends and family. The new headmaster at Therfield school honoured the word of Terry Reddin, the previous headteacher, and Abi and Becky were accepted back. Becky into A levels and Abi into GCSE's. A small team had got our house sorted in advance of us coming - cleaning, clearing and painting. We were very thankful.

Getting ready for school was the next challenge with school uniform etc. Elaine and Phil needed work. We had decided to take a break until Christmas to recharge ourselves; but for Elaine it was not to be. There was a teaching job at St Andrew's school from the September and the headteacher was very persuasive. It felt like it was God's provision at the time, though looking back, she maybe should have taken more time as she was back into teaching only ten days after we moved back to the UK.

Phil looked for any work he could find and managed to get a job delivering Yellow pages. Naively he took on three delivery rounds. He had to collect the yellow pages from the grounds of a pub in Esher. We filled the minibus and decided to go back for a second load. Phil was worried about the suspension. They filled a large part of our front room. What had he taken on? Delivering these books which were full size, not the size they are now, took four days with the help of all the family and others from another family. It was hard-earned money. Phil didn't do that again!

THE ROAD TO TRANSYLVANIA

CHAPTER 18

CRAFT ROMANIA AND FAIR TRADE (CRAFT UK)

(Written by Phil)

Before returning to England, I had investigated the idea of importing basket work from Romania. Bodrogi Csaba had introduced me to a few different families making willow baskets and corn brooms. The problem was, how would I get them transported from Romania?

Linda Harding had introduced us to a man from the Wirral that had a fair-trade shop and whose heart was for the marginalised, much like us. He had a van and often drove out to Albania to pick up goods. He agreed to go to Romania and pick up my first load. This was a very steep learning curve for me. I went on a 'Start your own business course' and VAT course and registered my business as Craft UK. Why UK? Because Bodrogi Csaba also had to register a business in Romania as Craft Romania so he could export for me and sort out all the export business in that country.

Romania was not in the EU then so there was a lot of red tape. Every basket had to be itemised, with a weight and purchase price. He then had to go to the Customs Office, with the loaded vehicle to get the mountain of paperwork for the export. I had to organise the import through Customs at Dover. What a palaver!

S-P's brother, Giles, had property near us with garages at the rear. We asked if he was able to help us with some space to store the baskets. He let us use one of the garages, half full of furniture. It was fine for what we needed at the start. It was very exciting unloading the first consignment. A great source of help and advice came from one of the Directors of Henry Gross Ltd - this was one of the two largest companies in the UK that imported willow products. He had a showroom in the basement of Proclamation House in Borough High Street where I had worked. His advice on many things was everything I needed. What an amazing connection!

The next question was, where was I going to sell the baskets? Again, God provided a connection with the Manager of The Swan Centre in Leatherhead. She had met leaders of our church at a meeting for significant people in Leatherhead when the

PHIL AND ELAINE INSIDE THE SWAN CENTRE, LEATHERHEAD

SELLING INSIDE THE SWAN CENTRE, LEATHERHEAD

church was looking to use the Theatre and help rejuvenate it and hopefully Leatherhead. She offered me a stall and a barrow on a Saturday in The Swan Centre, and the business began.

With the first consignment selling well, it was now time to take the plunge and go for larger order. Capital was needed, and some good friends came up with some interest-free loans. Our friends Kerry, Pat and Pete and Mary helped. The producers needed a deposit, as I will explain below, so they could purchase the willow, meaning that finance was needed for the imports in advance.

Having seen how the village producers were getting very little money for the excellent quality items they were producing locally, I looked at how we could agree a fair price with them and try and develop a market that brought them enough work. This took a lot of negotiation, and it was something that needed fine-tuning as the business developed. It was clear that they did not have the financial capability to purchase the raw products without a large deposit. An agreement was reached on the price of each item in Romanian currency (ROM). However, the changing currency rate with the pound becoming stronger against the ROM meant that each load became cheaper for me, but the producers had less money in their pocket. We then changed to a rate for each item in Sterling. Having agreed this rate, they would get the same price no matter the fluctuation of the pound in relation to the ROM.

Becky was doing her ICT A level and needed to design a web site. She designed it for the business, and that formed the basis of the website that ran for over ten years. I needed an e-mail address and help with setting up the computer for running my business. Another good friend of ours, Tim Rault-Smith helped with all this and arranged an e-mail account for me under his business host provider with the e-mail address of Craftuk.biz. God provided another contact who agreed to make it live with some additions, and he has administered the website all the way through.

Having a website meant that I could now look for wholesale outlets. One of my cousins who had connections with Mole Valley Farmers in the West Country organised a meeting with the buyer, and they decided to move over more ethical fair-traded baskets. They put me in touch with their distributor who agreed to take orders on behalf of Mole Valley Farmers and regular orders went directly to them from me for the various branches. Our faithful minibus was still our transport for the business. With seats taken out it served the purpose to begin with, but as orders increased, there was a need to look for alternatives. The size of the consignments from Romania also increased, and we had to use a Romanian distribution company that were delivering to a charity in Worthing. They agreed to unload and store our baskets until I could pick them up. This meant hiring a van, and Abi often came with me to load and bring the goods back to Cobham.

Guildford became the next venue for selling. It started when Rural Crafts offered me a space for the 10-day summer festival in June 2005. The problem was that each day we needed to set up in Guilford High Street then pack away the stall at the end of the day: we had half an hour to set up and unpack, before and after closing the street to traffic. Where was I going to keep stock, as the minibus only took a small amount along with the gazebo and tables? I was given the name of a man who managed a Christian Charity in Guildford and whose offices were at the top of the High Street. I spoke to him, and he invited me to look at what available space he had for the ten days I needed it. It was excellent and again was God's answer.

The website was doing its job and by advertising in The Wholesaler, it generated a lot of interest that including companies like Somerset levels. Fair trading shops and cycle shops became interested. We were marketing a unique product. Willow Baskets already appealed to many people as they were environmentally friendly. Willow is sustainable and decomposes when finished with, and we had the added bonus that this was Ethically Fair Traded too.

Having looked into The Fair-Trade International Policy I realised that the products could not be classed as Fair Trade in the Official sense. I obtained advice as how to set up an alternative Fair-Trade policy that we could agree on.

This policy, unlike The Fair-Trade International Policy, did allow children to be involved in the family production process on the basis that they were in full-time education – a very important part of passing on skills to children within a family.

This is the Fair-Trading Policy that was adopted.

TRADING POLICY

Craft Romania and Fair Trade (CRAFT) imports items on an Ethical and Fair Trade basis. Fair trade agreements with the producers have been agreed.

What does this mean?

As an Eastern European Country, Romania like many other Eastern European countries such as Albania is not classed as a Fair-Trade Country. However, many poor village craft producers in these countries struggle to survive, and many are at poverty level.

- **CRAFT** has developed an Ethical and Fair-Trading policy with a number of village communities in Central Romania.
- **CRAFT** pay 30% of the price of the product to the producers when placing an order and full payment on completion of order.
- **Children** are able and encouraged to work with their families in producing the goods as part of their culture, so they have the skills to continue the crafts. This would be in a home craft environment and not at a factory. This is not at the expense of school education. The families' children are expected to be involved in fulltime education and are encouraged to study for further education where appropriate.
- **CRAFT** knows the families personally.

CRAFT ROMANIA AND FAIR TRADE (CRAFT UK)

- **CRAFT** are looking to see Communities Transformed by firm trading agreements being established, giving stability and growth.
- **CRAFT** are strategically working with NGO's in Romania to provide support for these communities.

The next problem was extending our storage. Tim Poole agreed to give up one of his outbuildings to help with the storage. This was a great blessing but again became too small as the demand grew. Through a bizarre chain of phone calls, I eventually spoke with a man who had some storage space. I had seen an advert for storage and phoned the number which turned out to be the wrong one. The very sympathetic man, who had just taken over the phone number, wanted to know why I needed storage. He said he knew a friend who did have some storage space. So, I met this man in a lay-by near Send and we went to a field where there were some converted chicken sheds. He explained that he rented some space there but didn't need it all as his business was closing. He was willing to sublet to me at a very good rate. This became the main storage for the baskets though it was not without its problems due to damp in the winter. Another answer to prayer.

Importing using a forwarding company and part loads in Romanian transporters was not easy. It was also very frustrating at times, not knowing when they would arrive. Bodrogi Csaba introduced me to Miki Mircse who had a sprinter van and was willing to bring the goods to England. This was much easier, and he must have made twelve or more journeys for me. His van often came loaded, and soon that too became too small to take all the baskets ordered. He had to leave some behind. Again, an advert in a Romanian charity publication meant a phone call. It was advertising return space from Romania to England. I spoke to Chris Mutch on the phone, who had been taking Aid out to Romania since the Revolution. He became the answer to my transport problem and with the larger premises at Send, was able to deliver direct.

Things seemed to be going well. You did need to be energetic and in good health though to manage lots of lifting, packing and unpacking. No problem, I was very healthy, or that's what I thought. Sadly, in the winter of 2007 one of my cousins tragically died. I went to the funeral and afterwards at the wake, discussions turned to prostate cancer. Two of my other cousins who were there mentioned that they had been tested and found that they needed treatment. One of my cousins suggested I should be tested. I had no obvious symptoms and left it for a while but visiting my GP for something else I mentioned my cousins' discussion. It was my choice. If the PSA reading was high, it may not mean cancer and could bring undue concern I was told. I weighed it up and decided to have the test which proved positive. I had prostate cancer.

The consultant that I was referred to explained that the prostate needed to be removed and this could be by Robotic Surgery which he himself would do. Having recovered from the shock, I explained I was shortly driving out to Romania and would be away for about two weeks. This was not a problem and I was booked in to have the operation on my return. He said the recovery period would be fast although lifting heavy things should be limited for a while. How was the business going to continue? It did through friends and family. The now annual ten-day Guildford Craft festival was due to take place the next month. The operation was a success and the market stall took place. I was in attendance with Kerry, family, Tim Poole and Elaine's parents for a few days and others. They did the lifting and carrying. Praise God for my cousins mentioning to me about prostate cancer at that funeral. If they hadn't, it might have been someone else writing this book.

Romania coming into the EU had made importing so much easier. There was no need for custom papers anymore in Romania or at Dover and no import taxes. What was the business all about? It was designed to help the producers who were all from a Romany background to develop their trading and provide them with a good income. What difference did it make?

Speaking with this family after ten years of trading, Janos, the grandfather on the right in the photos below said, *"We have had nearly ten years, and we have got to know each other's families and have learnt to trust each other. It has made a big difference."*

One of his Grandsons, Loránd writes, *"I was probably 8 or 9 years old when my family met Phil Slade. The English man was living in Romania for several years and he intended to do business with my family; they are basket makers; his intention was to sell the baskets in England. At the beginning it was hard to believe*

FORGÁCS FAMILY

him; does he speak the truth? Is he to be trusted? Is he going to cheat us? But as weeks, months went by my family felt that he was a sincere man who was trying to help us, and this is how a nine-year-old partnership became a beautiful friendship. This really helped my family a lot and two years ago I was even able to help him to sell the baskets in England. It was a great to work together. Best of all is that the money earned from the business went to the charity to help poor people not for him. I have learned so much from him; he is a great example."

The business grew with a wholesale customer base of about forty. It could have easily grown with the right marketing and resources, but without employing someone and finding larger storage space, we monitored growth carefully. Gabor Istvan (Ösci) came to live with us. He helped me a lot with markets for eighteen months, but Kerry was our main helper. She tried to be at every market. Despite being a full-time practice nurse, she took holiday time off to try and be available. I am not sure how we could have continued without her help and the continued help of my girls and my wife when she was free.

KERRY AT A MARKET IN KENT

Many young people came to England; before the EU this was very hard with lots of red tape and restrictions. Judith came and looked after my Stepmother, Janet. I'm not sure if Janet could have stayed in her home if Judith had not been there to help. Many of the young people we see as our extended family and Judith is one of these.

Markets became bigger and more frequent, travelling across the country as far as the Yorkshire Showground. The markets in Guildford continued, and I attended the Craft market at Christmas as well as some Saturdays throughout the year on the Bridge near Debenhams. These markets had for many years been run by Colin Styles and had become a feature of City. As the stall was becoming known and generated a lot of interest and support, I was allowed to become part of the regular Tuesday Farmers' Market in Guildford.

GÁBOR ISTVÁN (ÖCSI) AT TOWER BRIDGE

Loránd who writes above is the grandson of one of the families that I had seen grow up, was now reaching 18. In Romania, a minor is not allowed to travel abroad unless a parent or an adult who must have papers signed by a Notary accompanies them. I had just been asked to do a Christmas Market at Loseley Manor, near Guildford and was offered extra space at a vastly reduced price if I had a demonstrator. While I was visiting the family, I felt I should ask Loránd if he would like to come to England and demonstrate for me. He could not hide a big smile and after agreeing with his parents. I booked the flights. He was coming!

Loránd arrived on his first visit to England - he seemed relieved to see me at Luton. His first time flying. Traffic driving on the other side. Three lane motorways. Miles, not kilometres. I think culture shock kept him quiet as I drove in the rush hour traffic back to Cobham. He had a day to acclimatise as the market set up was the next day. Chris (my new transport solution) had brought willow, his tools and working board. We loaded this into the van with the stock and off we went to Loseley. Kerry, Loránd and I unloaded and set up ready for a four-day market. His understanding of English was quite good, but he was very shy about speaking in case he got it wrong. He got on with the family very well and he seemed surprised how much people appreciated him. Our multicultural society wasn't lost on him. In Romania, there is still prejudice against the darker skin of the Romany people. Here it was different. His confidence grew and by the end of the market, he was smiling and trying to answer questions from the public rather than pointing them in my direction first.

Loránd was eager to come back, and we found sponsorship for him to return to England in September 2014 and attend Guilford College one evening a week. He helped me with the business, and his English became very good. He passed his Level 1 English as a Second Language course, and he had improved so well he was asked to go to Level 2. He went round the country with me delivering baskets and enjoyed a trip to Merseyside to see my elderly Aunt on the Wirral, the ferry across the Mersey and of course, The Cavern to experience the history of The Beatles.

LORÁND AT GUILDFORD MARKET

LORÁND IN LIVERPOOL

CHAPTER 19

CLOSURE OF THE BUSINESS AND SZTOIKA CSABA

(Written by Phil)

Little did we know when we had arranged for Loránd to come and live with us in September, our close friend, Kerry who was part of our family for over thirty years, would be diagnosed with two brain tumours in June 2014. This was a big shock to us all, and Loránd immediately became my right-hand man.

Having successfully completed his first term at Guildford College, he passed his exam and was asked to go up to Level Two from the next term. Sadly, during that Christmas, while he was home in Romania, his younger brother, Boti aged 8 years old, was diagnosed with Leukaemia and Loránd made the decision to stay and not come back. The decision was based on the consultant's opinion that if his brother, Boti was to have the best chance, he must stay happy and Loránd told me that he was staying to try and keep his brother happy. A number of people started to pray for his brother. He went through a lot of treatment, always with Loránd beside him as much as possible. There seem to have been many miracles in this lad's life, and he has now finished most of his treatment and is doing very well.

Things were becoming increasingly clear that the season for the business was drawing to a close. I had real problems with dry storage. The human resources needed to continue with the business was putting a great strain on the family with both Kerry and Loránd not being around in 2015. I had spoken with the producers in the previous October and said that the business would probably finish. We had over ten years together and it had made a great difference to their families – the dream that God had given me in starting the business had been fulfilled.

I was looking to bring the business to a close in April 2015 but a lad, Sztoika Csaba got in touch with me. I will call him Sztoika which is his family name as Csaba is such a common Christian name. For those unfamiliar with the Hungarian culture, the surname always proceeds the Christian name.

Sztoika was one of the lads that we were very close to as a family in the camps, leading up to us going to Romania and while we were living there. When he graduated, we stepped in as parents for him at school. We also secured sponsorship for him to complete university. Sztoika was always interested in business and has a heart for the people group he was part of. Interestingly, he had come with on my first visit to a Gypsy village to see if they were interested in making things for me. He was there at the beginning of my relationship with the basket work producers in Siménfalva/Simonesti and loaded one of the first vans with me in Romania.

His artistic skills also developed as he made clay models, many of which were displayed in homes both in Romania and England. He lived in Marosvásárhely/Targu Mures for a while and attended ethical business conferences connected to

Opportunity Romania and our connections with SP, Paztor Feri and Szabo Istvan.

He was always interested in doing business using ethical principles which he picked up from seminars he attended while we were in Romania. He was influenced by people who wanted the best for him. His English and German language were good and after we had left Romania he went to live at a monastery in Germany where he learnt a great deal.

One day, Sztoika phoned me saying that he wanted to be in partnership with me and start a business in Germany. His ideas were that he mirrored my operation in the UK, importing willow products to Germany and other EU countries. It seemed interesting that this came at a time I was looking to cease trading. Was this another part of God's plan?

I agreed to meet him in Hannover in February 2015, and he told me all his ideas. It was not just willow products; he had a host of other projects he wanted to work on too.

The year of 2015 brought a lot of change. I was now working alongside Csaba Sztoika and visiting both Germany and Romania on a number of occasions. Many samples were made by Siménfalva/Simonesti for Csaba to try, and also other producers in Romania made samples.

Here are just a few statistics of baskets sold in the UK from the village producers of Harghita. They did an amazing amount of work! We also worked with many skilled people, especially in woodwork, reed and wooden earrings.

PRODUCT (NUMBER SOLD)

Laundry/Linen Baskets	(1,900)
Log Trug baskets	(1,400)
Log baskets	(3,000)
Treasure baskets	(5,500)
Storage baskets and display baskets	(7,770)
Shopping baskets	(5,570)
Total number of items sold altogether	**(52,962)**

Sadly, Kerry, who had been the main support in the business, was suffering from a terminal illness and died in August 2015. She was loved by our family. Kerry had supported us through all the stages of family life, including delivering both Becky and Abi into the world. Her wish was that donations at her Thanksgiving service be given to Heart for Romania for its continued work with marginalised people in Transylvania.

This book is dedicated to her.

KERRY WITH OUR FAMILY

THE ROAD TO TRANSYLVANIA

PART TWO

Perspectives

THE ROAD TO TRANSYLVANIA

CHAPTER 20

ELAINE

"We're going to live in Romania" were the first words my husband said as we met him at the airport after he helped to lead a summer camp in that country. It had been his first time in Romania and due to lack of mobile signal there, this was the first communication we had had since he left two weeks before. I am usually the one who invites adventure as my family will tell you, whilst my husband adds balance with his cautionary nature. So, this was a bolt out of the blue and rather unnerving as it came out of nowhere.

I should have known really, as this had been preceded two years before in 1996 by our eldest daughter, Anne, uncharacteristically accepting an invitation to be part of a summer camp for children from the huge Orphanage in Cristuru Secuiesc, a town in the Harghita County of Romania. Anne had always been a home bird and as a young child had been shy of new people, that isn't to say she didn't have spirit, but she liked being with family. It was amazing to watch my daughter discover her own personal faith in God through her experiences out there, and she wrote some wonderful poems which expressed how deep this experience had been for her. I naturally thought this experience was my daughter's and that for us a family, it would stop there.

After her second camp, Anne badgered Phil to go with her the next year. Eventually, he gave in and said he would go on two conditions. First, work would give him unpaid leave (which was unlikely). Second, he would go in a supporter role rather than as a leader. I was full-time teaching by then, so our holidays were precious with the girls and he did not feel it right to give up two of his five weeks at that time. We laid these conditions as a fleece before God. Miraculously, God fulfilled those conditions and things were looking the way Phil wanted them; however, have you ever had God alter things according to His plans at times such as these? Two days before the trip started one of the leaders broke his leg and couldn't go, so Phil was asked to step in and help lead! This was probably God's saving grace for Phil as he is much more a leader than a follower!

I have to admit, I thought Phil's passion shown in abundance as he met us at the airport, would ebb away slowly and that we would stay settled in Cobham. It was too much of a lifetime upheaval to contemplate; besides God had not said a word to me about it. Phil's passion did not recede, and often he would sit and cry for the children he had helped care for on the camp; for those young lives who were part of an institution rather than a family. My thoughts reflected back to when we were newly married when we thought we had heard a calling to South America. The door had closed to that plan, but we had both pursued it until it had. Then my mind wandered to later years when we had heard a calling from God to move from the East end of London to the Isle of Skye. We had uprooted ourselves from the church and neighbourhood in which we had both grown up and prepared the family for a significant change together. The door to that plan slammed shut six weeks before we were due to move. Those doors had closed; so why would we spend time exploring another one when one of us had not received the call? I was open but nothing came; it remained a mystery.

Phil was keen that the whole family should experience Romania and see for themselves. He was so persistent that we spent a month there the next summer in 1999, having a holiday for two weeks and leading a camp for the other two weeks. Looking back, I am surprised that I agreed, our youngest two were 9 and 11 years old, and I had no idea what they would be exposed to there. The whole thing seemed foreign and alien to me. After all, my knowledge of Romania from childhood had mostly been the tales of Richard Wurmbrand imprisoned for his faith behind the iron curtain. Since the Revolution in 1990, the media portrayed it as a land left ravaged by the communists, riddled with corruption and overflowing with parentless children.

We travelled overland in our faithful blue VW minibus to Romania, through several countries, each with their own currency at that time. It was a veritable adventure way beyond anything we had experienced as a couple yet alone as a family. We stayed in youth hostels, mostly in a six-bed dormitory so we could be together; therein lies more stories which are often recounted amongst the family even today. Phil, Anne and the younger two girls got more excited with every border we crossed bringing us closer to Romania, whilst Rachel our second daughter and I grew more apprehensive and nervous. In due course, we crossed the frontier into Romania. Here we found a land which bore a resemblance to the United Kingdom in the 1950s. The main form of transport was horse and cart; there were few if any, mobile phones and the fields of harvest were being cut with a scythe. Somehow though, it was reassuring rather than disconcerting.

Our first two weeks were a baptism of fire; with no creature comforts as we camped out with the children. It was a twenty-four-hour responsibility, with virtually no privacy. Our children lived side by side with children and teenagers from a vastly different background and upbringing to their own, and yet, I had to give the girls to God and believe He walked with them through these experiences. The children from the Orphanage, or Children's Home as we preferred to call it, were affectionate and hungry to be loved and cared for. This was something that both Phil and I could do as we were naturally, *children people*.

We then spent two weeks in a village called Tăureni at the other end of the valley. Again, God broke into our plans at this time in a way that we could not have premeditated or foreseen for ourselves. Looking back as a mother, I had no idea at the time of how a chance meeting at the end of our time in Romania would be a lifeline for us as a family when we moved out there. After all, I still had not received a call! We encountered a family who lived a few doors down from the motel where we stayed. The husband had taught himself English to an impressive level and his ability to converse with us was like music to our ears, and true to Székely hospitality we were having dinner with his family two hours later. Although we only saw them once or twice, a natural bond developed quickly between both families.

I cannot say that the month in Romania had confirmed that we should live there, which was disappointing for Phil and Anne. However, they were undeterred and continued to talk in terms of "when" we live in Romania rather than "if" we move to Romania. My own strivings ceased after a conversation with a dear friend, Linda Harding, who was walking the journey with us. I explored with her the fact that I did not feel called to Romania. Linda asked me, "What has God put on your heart to do?" That was easy; I knew I had been called early on in my teaching career, amongst other things, to bind up broken-hearted children. Linda gazed at me with amusement and asked me, "what will you be doing in Romania?" All at once I got it. God, through Linda, had given me the calling I needed to move things forward.

Now it was the children's turn to be called. Both Phil and I had always included our children and were adamant that this was not going to be something that was done to them. The call to us had to be tested by our children too. Becky was uncertain for a long time, but we waited patiently. Rachel decided to remain in the UK with friends to finish her A levels. This was so hard as a mother, and it tested my faith that God would take care of her for me. Becky then felt God say to her that it was going to be alright. She surprised us one morning at breakfast by saying, "It's okay, we can go to Romania. God's told me it's going to be alright "

We began to air our thoughts with the elders of our church; we were true pioneers, as no-one had asked before to be sponsored to go abroad. We met a fair amount of resistance and eventually, in November 1999, we decided to lay the dream down. If God wanted it to happen, He would have to make it happen. What happened next is detailed in this book.

Eighteen months later in August 2001, we moved to Romania with Rachel, Becky and Abi. Rachel had felt so unsettled that she had prayed again and realised she had made her decision on what she thought was expected of her rather than listening to the call - a lesson for all of us. We did face criticism that we were ruining our children's education, but the call by now was so strong that we knew God would intercede in this for us.

I decided to home school Becky and Abi, who were both secondary age now, through an online Christian school attached to a real life school in Manchester - we completed assignments through them after I taught the girls the content. It was new ground for me, but after we all worked through the fact that their mum was also their teacher, I loved it and managed to teach them all the years up to GCSE level. God was faithful and blessed both the younger girls with successful academic education at university in later years, as well as the added bonus of a rich cultural education in a very different country to their own.

Some of the challenges in the first year, as well as the obvious ones of language and culture, were freezing conditions for almost six months, us as a family being together all day every day, and the lack of privacy in a culture where doors are always unlocked for neighbours to enter. I had some medical challenges due to frequent infections and breaking my coccyx when sliding down abruptly on the ice. Nonetheless, we were surrounded by neighbours and friends who put people rather than things first. The Székely people were incredibly hospitable and supportive, from learning the language to acquiring a telephone and internet line.

I tried hard to live as they did, learning to cook dishes and preserve pickles and make spreads for winter provision from my now close friend Bodrogi Kati, the wife of the man who spoke fluent English in 1999. Bodrogi Csaba was a lifeline to Phil as he got to grips with the Romanian culture whilst trying to help the young people leaving the Children's home to find jobs and flats. We had a 'open home' and frequently a meal for the five of us would end up feeding ten of us as the young people turned up at lunchtime. Our relationships with many young people grew, and we tried our best to show them that we cared for them with what language we had. Linda had been right; I was in my element being *mum* to tens of young people. They began to call us "mum and dad" and the girls their "sisters."

It was challenging but fulfilling; heart-breaking at times but satisfying at others. We literally walked life with them. We were involved with roughly two hundred children and young people. Of this number, sixty regularly came to our house and of that number, twenty literally became part of our extended family. Our daughters were amazing; they freely shared us with the young people. This was the benefit of having been called as a family. We were in this together, and in their own way they cared for and were Christian role models for the young people too.

Before we went, a friend had told me during a time of prayer that being a mum was pivotal to our life out there, and indeed it was so. Phil worked mainly with the young people, interacting with businesses and representatives in the local community, and I taught the girls and ran the home. We often had young people in our house during the day or staying over and sometimes living with us, which meant a juggling act with the girls' education. The lack of privacy was an issue we had to address eventually in order to stay united and sane as a family. We went to stay one weekend a month in a retreat centre in Brașov; this proved to be a real blessing and an absolute lifesaver.

We lived life on the edge; it was exciting but exhausting at times. We knew times of miraculous provision and of miraculous protection or help. Whenever we were in need of help or support, it would come just at the right time. We witnessed soup cooked for six of us provide ample sustenance for ten or twelve people - money suddenly appearing in an impoverished bank balance - diesel lasting for an extraordinary amount of miles - an interpreter as before unknown, turning up at a crucial moment. Then there was the miraculous provision every time we had a medical issue whether it was an emergency or an everyday concern. We had a vital link with a Doctor, Lorincz

Csaba, at the local hospital who spoke English who could not have done more for us than he did. He was amazingly patient and gracious and often went the second mile, connecting us with other professionals if we needed it. I had a nasty accident in the third year and split my lip open badly during a fall. Lorincz Csaba responded immediately, and within an hour my lip was being sewn up by the only face surgeon in the County, resulting in a perfectly healed scar with minimal impact to my appearance.

We invested in language lessons with a local priest, Gereb Laci, and spent much of our first six months studying it and studying the culture which was vastly different to the UK. This opened up the way to communicate appropriately with Hungarian speaking people. Our good friends the Bodrogi family helped us enormously in this way, patiently explaining how best to say things and gently pointing out if we had made a cultural error. The girls and I were conversant after the first year. Phil frustratingly found it harder to grasp the rudiments of the language, although he understands most conversations now.

One of the greatest blessings was the company God provided along this journey; friendships with other families and couples living in the area, some indigenous and some from abroad serving in Harghita. These people became very dear to us and without whom our lives would have been far more difficult. Those close friendships still remain long after leaving Romania. They helped to soften the hardship of living away from our family in England, especially through times of illness or the death of a loved one. Phil's dad died during our second year there, but again miraculously I had been home due to medical issues and had realised that Phil needed to come home to see his father quickly, so he was able to say goodbye. It was hard at first to be together as a family 24/7; but we quickly became conscious that this was a special season in our lives and that we would possibly never have it again, so we made it work.

In Chapter 4, we copied some thoughts from my journal, quoting, "Year one was great. Making relationships, opening our home, learning the language, getting used to the culture." If the first year had been a time of wonder, this is what I wrote about the second year. "Year two was sheer blood and guts. Such a difficult year – deepening relationships, disciplining, finding jobs, having to persevere as the youngsters gave up at things, no privacy at all – burn out. No Rachel – this made a big difference." Rachel had gone back to university in the UK.

At the end of year two, it was very interesting as those youngsters that we had been closest to went to work or university in other towns, countries or had been called into the Army. The strangest thing, despite the blood, sweat and tears of the second year and many of the young people we knew best moving away, we had a definite call to stay for a third year. We knew we hadn't finished what we had gone to do but weren't sure exactly what that looked like. Also, we had to depend on sponsorship from family and friends as both HfR and our church could no longer support us financially. They had committed for two years, but we were staying for a third. Of course, we saw another absolute miracle of God's provision; the money given to us went further!

In the third year, God found an indigenous godly couple who moved to our house to continue the work we were doing, which had been one of our greatest desires. We didn't want to abandon the young people who were around us but on the other hand, we knew that at some point they would have to live life independently; we couldn't bail them out forever. It was hard as they were like extended family to us. Of course, little did we know, as the border laws were different then, that many would follow us to England in later years and make life there. This wasn't what we intended, as our belief was that they should remain in their own country but after Romania joined the European Union job opportunities decreased dramatically for young people from their background. They have all built up a life for themselves; we feel grateful that we had a small part in preparing them for life. By staying the third year, we were able to put things in place to leave a legacy of care for the young people, which then continued to give them the confidence later to make big decisions in life.

Yes, of course there were times when we were young peopled out. There were times of frustration as we sought the appropriate words in a foreign language. In it all, we knew we had been called and God had provided for us in every way. We lacked for nothing; that's not to say we lived a life of luxury, but we had enough to live on and to bless others too. In fact, very often when we gave away what we had in faith that God would provide for us, it would return to us in some way and frequently it was a double portion.

Not everything was rosy; there were times when I wondered if God knew what He was doing with my family; the sacrifice seemed too great at times. Would I do it again as a mother? Most definitely. Those experiences taught me that my children are cared for much more passionately by God than I could ever care for them, even with my fiercely protective motherly feelings. It stood me in good stead for a future in which my daughters have followed and continue to follow God's leading into places and experiences that naturally I as mother, would want to shield them from.

CHAPTER 21

ANNE

Our Romanian adventure started when Tim Poole asked Mum and Dad if they thought that I would be interested in going on a summer camp to Romania when I was just 14. They thought that I would turn it down as I was such a home bird, but I didn't. I think I surprised them when I said that I would love to go. I hadn't really thought much about the new culture that I would experience or what we were expected to do once we got there.

ANNE

We were required to meet as a team a few times before we went out. These were times of great fun and really helped us to bond before we left. I remember wondering how I could be involved and feeling that I didn't really have any talents or gifts that were suitable. Shash looked at my tie-dye t-shirt and friendship bracelets and asked if I had made them myself; these were to be the activities which I would lead on the camp.

I had flown before to Austria, but I remember the sheer excitement and novelty of flying without my parents this time. When we arrived at Bucharest airport, we queued up to buy our visas at the passport desk and then passport control. The officers refused to speak English. One of our team members was taken off into a strip search room and asked for a bribe to be released; our first encounter with corruption.

We piled into the minibus, suitcases and all. It was a long way to Erzsébet Kút (our campsite). We wound up through the Carpathian Mountains close to Bran (where Dracula is supposed to have lived). I was amazed by the picture-perfect scenes of snow-capped mountains, steam trains chugging through the valleys and luscious green trees everywhere. We stopped on the way at a small spring to fill up our water bottles, straight out of a tap in the mountain. I remember being surrounded at one point by men with long black moustaches reaching below their shoulders and tall hats. There were pretty girls with pigtails down to their waists, tied with red ribbons. I later learned that these were Roma gypsies.

We drove through Székelykeresztúr/Cristuru Secuiesc, where the Children's Home was situated and arrived at the bottom of the campsite. We were mobbed by children who stroked our faces, gazed at our pale skin and held our hands as we began the long windy ascent to the campsite. The older boys loaded themselves up like donkeys and ran up the steep steps to the top carrying our heavy luggage. A campfire was being prepared in the corner, as we dumped our suitcases inside our tiny two-man tents. I was desperate for the toilet, so was shown into the woods by a group of around ten children. The

WC consisted of a shack stuck over a hole in the ground which has been dug out by one of the older boys and then covered in lime powder. It stank! "Oh well," I thought, "I better get used to this as I am here for two weeks." I think that this was the first time that I felt a real excitement at having to make the most of a situation and turning it into an adventure.

By the end of my first week on camp, I had fallen in love with the children from the orphanage and with the Székely people of Romania. I felt that I had finally found a place that I could call my second home.

The following summer, I returned to Romania with a different team and this second experience confirmed my love for the country and in particular the Székely people. It was whilst I was on this camp in 1997 that an amazing angelic encounter took place. One day, we had set off on a walk with the kids up the mountain behind the campsite. Halfway up, I felt wheezy and knew that I had to turn back to get my inhaler. One of the older boys insisted on coming back down with me, but I explained that I would be fine as I could see the campsite clearly from where we were. So, I set off on my own.

Little did I realise that once I began the descent that the campsite would not be so clearly in my view. Next, a storm began to brew, and it tipped down with rain; thunder boomed, and lightning struck a tree close to me. I was petrified and called out to God to help me but the more I cried, the more alone I felt. Suddenly I saw a shadow move behind a tree; I had just seen a flock of sheep grazing so assumed that it was a shepherd. The next thing I knew was a hand on my shoulder. I peered up to see a tall man with dark hair. His face was bright and glowing. I tried to communicate to him that I was lost and needed to get back to camp. He didn't say a word but smiled. I took his arm and within minutes we were back at the campsite. When I turned around to thank him, he had vanished. This surely was an angel. I still feel a tingle in my heart when I think about it.

The following year, I managed to convince Dad to come out on a summer camp with me. It was so special to be able to share my passion with my Dad and sure enough, this special country captured his heart too. The kids on the camp loved my Dad too. I felt so privileged and blessed to have him as my Dad, watching him tell jokes and befriend the older boys who saw him as a father figure - and many still do to this day.

After I had finished secondary school and applied for teacher training college, I decided to take a gap year and headed back to Romania. For the first few months, I joined a team from Poplars Church in Worksop who were living in Sânpetru just outside Brașov. It was very different being in the Romanian speaking part of Romania, and living in a huge city had its challenges. Every day, we would take the bumpy bus ride into the centre of town; in the winter months, the hard bus seats were so cold that we used to sit on our hands.

There was such a divide between the rich and the poor classes, and I really struggled with this. I clearly remember walking over a grate by the huge shopping mall in town and catching a glimpse of a homeless boy sitting in the sewer below the grate, sniffing a plastic bag of glue. He looked up at me and in that moment, my heart melted in compassion. The policemen in the city often mistreated the street kids if they were seen in public places.

Most of my time in Brașov was spent in a large Baby and Children's Orphanage. I found the conditions very upsetting but felt privileged to be able to help in some way and bring a little light into a dark place. These experiences opened my eyes to the more sensitive and darker parts of the country that I loved. I drew on the feelings that were evoked to write many poems. This helped to process the reality of what I saw on a daily basis at the orphanage. One day in particular, stands out in my mind, never to be forgotten. It was a sunny morning, as I arrived at the orphanage gates. The security guard hadn't arrived yet, and I looked down and saw a small bundle by the gate. To my surprise, the small bundle was a new-born baby. She must have been only a few weeks old. Often mothers would leave their babies at the gates of the orphanage and watch from the corner until they were collected. I took the baby into the Director's office and she asked me to name her: I named her, Ioana (Joanna in English).

I then went on to spend the rest of the year in Székelykeresztúr, which continued to shape me as a young woman and challenge me in many ways. These experiences were faith-building and acted as a platform for my mission experiences later on the MV Doulos. My eyes had been opened to a world full of joy yet sadness, desperate fear yet hope, and I felt like I had broken out of my comfort zone and started on my own journey through life.

THE ROAD TO TRANSYLVANIA

CHAPTER 22

RACHEL

When I heard my family was off to live in Romania, it was no surprise. We had heard stories and seen pictures from Anne throughout the past three years since her first visit. Then once Dad went on camp to Romania and we also visited, it seemed that Romania was mentioned all the time.

There were key people in Pioneer People who encouraged us as children and then as youth, to think beyond the borders of our own country. Linda Harding was a key mentor, who had been in Pioneer People before moving to Japan. She invited Becky and I to visit her there. At the age of 15, this was to be one of my first encounters with God putting the seed and passion in my heart for the Nations.

RACHEL

I think looking back that this got my heart and head in gear for my year in Romania. It meant that when the decision was made, it felt almost a natural thing to be part of it. Even at this young age, I remember wanting to break the mould of normality but needing confirmation that it was acceptable to do this.

When my parents said that moving to Romania was definitely going ahead, reality hit. I was going to need to decide whether to stay or go! My parents didn't try to persuade me either way; they wanted me to make the decision. To stay would mean to finish my A levels, and I felt that was the expected thing to do. To go would mean to go on an adventure with my family and stepping into the excitement of the unknown. The second sounded more exciting, but the first seemed sensible. I decided to do the sensible thing and remain in school.

After I had come to this decision, I became anxious and distracted. I had difficulty sleeping and looking back I thought that I needed to put my head down and not engage too much with the Romania vision, but life as I knew it. The plan was simple; I would get through my A levels, and then revisit my dreams and passions. Things didn't go according to plan. I was miserable and received poor grades on my AS levels. My Mum came into my room one day and quietly sat with me until I finished my next frustrated outburst at not being able to concentrate on my homework. I remember she very gently reminded me that Romania was my decision, and that decision could change at any time as I felt led. She suggested that I prayed and that there would be no harm in silently deciding that I would go to Romania and just see how I felt. She had seen the inner turmoil within me.

Prayer was a regular part of our family life, even praying for weather on rainy bank holidays when we were off to the sea. This type of prayer, praying my own prayers and making a big decision based on God speaking to me, seemed daunting. So, I just prayed that God would give me peace if it was right to go.

With this prayer, I silently decided to change my mind and go to Romania. I didn't hear God audibly, but the weight that fell off my shoulders and the relief that swept over me could not be mistaken. I slept so well that night!

Something I greatly appreciate is the fact that space was given for me to make the decision and that the decision could be changed. It mirrors the heart of God in wanting a relationship with us as individuals. He is patient and lets us explore how He speaks to us, not reprimanding us for needing time or trying different avenues but releasing us and letting us work out His best. I will also add here that the fact that I was given the choice, meant that when things were tough, I would always go back and remember I freely chose to go. I never blamed my parents when things were hard, but gained peace leaning more on my relationship with Jesus than ever before.

From the moment I arrived in Romania, I realised that for me, the Székely people were a perfect match with my extrovert nature. My days were taken up with preparing food, cleaning the house and other household chores, but this was rarely done alone. Actually, I very rarely remember doing anything on my own there. I remember one day having worked my way through preparing a ridiculous number of apples from our back garden, coring them, cutting out the bad bits and getting to the last one when another washing up bowl full appeared. Marcella, a good friend arrived just as I was looking at the next bowl in despair. She rolled up her sleeves and said as more of a statement than a question that she could help. As we began Sanyi then turned up, another good friend and just joined in without any words.

I regularly walked the thirty-minute journey into Udvarhely to get our shopping accompanied by whoever may have been at our house at that time. The walk would be full of conversation and stories. On an icy day, of which there were many in winter, the black ice, often had me on my back before I knew it! I would look up at their worried faces, which would amuse me and then laughter would follow with them retelling the story multiple times with actions and facial expressions. They would then stay for lunch, as they knew they were always welcome.

This was what I loved about Romania. We had gone to be family, to just be and see how we could journey with the people there. They warmly welcomed us to do just that and loved living life with us too. We ate together, worked together, walked together, sang together, and played together. The list was endless. Their own agenda was not important. If the opportunity was there to be involved in whatever was going on, that's what they would do. Their attitude conveyed that coring apples was just as fun as playing volleyball, BUT only when it was with someone else. They were like my siblings, and I loved them as such.

The house was almost always filled with noise and laughter. Our friends added to the noise, but we ourselves are a pretty loud family and it doesn't take much to get us laughing. Many times, our giggles had to be stifled among ourselves when cultural or language mispronunciations occurred.

Being served pig brain soup was an early encounter, which we were not quite ready for, especially as the brain was floating in the top of the soup and actually looked like brain. I have to say it is actually delicious, but just the idea of what we were about to eat made us girls a little twitchy. Dad was deeply engrossed in conversation, so as I was sitting next to him, I subtly scooped the brain out of my own soup and popped it into Dad's. Becky saw this and followed suit, promptly putting the brain from her soup into mine. I silently showed my dismay shooting daggers at her. Becky looked at me with triumph then went to resume eating her own soup only to find more brain in her own soup. What Becky had not seen was that at the same time she was triumphantly looking at me, Abi had put her pig brain into Becky's soup. I still remember her disbelieving look trying to work out where the brain had come from, which then caused a stifled giggle from Abi and me. Becky soon caught on, and the war was on as to who was going to end up with the most amount of brain in their soup. Mum was silently trying to reprimand us, while pig brain was subtly being passed back and forth between bowls. In the end, Dad seemed the easiest target and ended up with the brain pieces from all our soups, as he was still fully engrossed in his conversation with our hosts. It was only when Dad had come to the end of his conversation that he began again on his soup. He looked down with disbelief at the expanded tower of pig brain in his bowl. At this point I excused myself for the toilet and we girls, including Mum, ran out of opposite doors averting our eyes to avoid an explosion of laughter! Dad was a hero; he ate it all! I now love pig brain soup thanks to the wonderful Bodrogi Kati!

Laughing with the Székely people came naturally to us all. When the language and cultural differences were different, laughter broke all barriers that may have been up before. It made learning Hungarian easier and more fun – laughing at myself around others and not being afraid to get the language totally wrong. The time when I asked at a posh restaurant totally innocently and politely, or so I thought, where I could take a p***, left the whole table and waitress roaring with laughter. I suppose there were some drawbacks of learning a language mostly from the youth.

I had formed a close friendship with many of the youth, and in a short period of time they wanted to converse with me past, "How are you?" One day, a friend who spoke the best English said that she and others wanted to talk to me about their stories and more personal issues, but they couldn't while I only knew limited Hungarian. To my horror, she then said that she had decided that she would no longer talk to me in English only Hungarian! This was my motivation for learning the language and as I was with the youth most days, I picked the language up quickly.

When returning to England after my year in Romania I had very little, if any debriefing and returned to a place that had once been my community with a thriving church, incredible friends and family. My entry back was hard. The town was socially desolate. Most of my friends were at university or had moved away. Looking back, the Coleman family and Kerry Stephens were the people God had placed in that area for me so that I did not totally collapse. The grief, however, of leaving the place I loved in Romania and the family and people I loved, left me feeling completely isolated and alone. I knew I had been called to be a nurse, and my training was the reason I came home, but I had not realised the pain of loss I would need to go through leaving my family in Romania. I moved to the University in Chelmsford, which was near my Aunty, Uncle and cousins, who were also lifelines for me at this time. My oldest sister, Anne and grandparents were further up north, and we would try to see them when possible, although with my shifts and distance it was not always easy.

My time spent in Romania was a mixed bag of experiences, ranging from exciting and full of adventure to tough and feeling out of my depth in many situations, including culturally. This has all taken a long time to process, which may have been sped up had there been an extended time of debriefing to help me unpick things earlier. I have since realised these experiences moulded and shaped me into who I am today, deepening my relationship with Jesus. How did my story turn out as it did? I took a leap of faith, talked to God regularly, worked hard through the difficult stuff and found He is faithful. This gives me confidence for my future. I can trust Him, He is my constant companion and wherever my adventures lead me next my home remains in Him.

HELPFUL THOUGHTS

Below are some thoughts that could be helpful, particularly for teenage children in similar positions.

Importance of a mentor for each child (particularly for teenagers). Being asked the big questions and seeing what is going well and what is not going so well by an older person, not your parents.

Visits from friends and church members. It restored us every time.

Family/team time. Regroup without those of different cultures, doing something fun and talking together. Our holidays to Brașov and other areas were vital.

One-to-one time with parents and children (if in a family). Parents making time to hear of struggles as well as victories, keeps clear communication between parents and children. Also, when parents are being shared with others, it allows their own children to feel loved.

Debriefing. Crucial! To have someone sit down and talking through your time, helps begin the process of sorting and understanding your own thoughts and feelings.

Clear boundaries for teenagers. Particularly discussed before and during the period of time there. Due to culture and language, edges can become blurred in a foreign country. Although a child wants freedom at that age, close guidance is needed and open communication.

Contact with those back home. When older children are back home, my parent's regular texts, calls and emails were invaluable.

CHAPTER 23

BECKY

I was sharing with someone about our open house in Romania, and how on some days, we welcomed fifty or sixty young people into our home who called Mum and Dad, "mum and dad." He was shocked and said, "How did you feel about that, sharing your parents with so many others?" "I loved it; it made me happy to know I could share my parents with others who needed them." Saying it, I realised that part of the reason behind my love was that we as children had been part of this decision to go and be family to these young people.

My parents had asked us if God had called each of us to Romania. When He revealed to each of us that He did, we were in. Looking back, I can see how this played such a vital part of the way in which Abi and I adjusted to life in Romania. I felt part of what my parents were doing and called

BECKY

to, not just being taken. They felt called and knew God had called us as a family, but they waited patiently and trusted God to speak to us each individually before really making the final decision. It took a while for me to open my ears to hearing God's voice, but my parents waited patiently for me to know God's peace in it.

It wasn't quite like this from the beginning though. When you are 11 years old and your Dad comes back from a short-term mission trip, the scariest thing to hear him say is, "We're going to move to Romania." Not, "Hello, how was your week?" Dad had changed, and it was a bit unnerving to say the least. Usually, Dad is the only one in our family (apart from Abi) who is in control of a situation. He's the one who thinks through things logically and comes up with all the possible pitfalls of a decision before taking action. Yet, here he was, spontaneous and wild as the rest of us, driven by this calling God had given him. It made no sense to us. After Mum was also on board, I thought I had better start asking God for a sense of peace and calling, as Dad's passion had not dwindled. I want to thank my parents that we were part of the decision as it showed how they valued us, our faith and our opinions. What a privilege to be children of these giants in faith who stepped out into the darkness waiting for God to turn the light on.

Those three years in Romania, from age 13 to 16, were key steps towards adult life. The journey has enriched my life more than any other experience could have. I learnt many new things, some practical, some spiritual, some emotional. Let me share with you a few of these.

When living in any new culture, there are of course many new practical things you learn. We made many close friends with the locals and so naturally, as they did what was normal everyday things for them, they taught us these things. In the autumn we learnt the secrets of the Székely people's winter diet. This involved how to make pickles, delicious chargrilled vegetable spreads, interesting ways of preserving fruit and meats; all things that were impossible to get hold of during the long cold winter days. Mum had a fierce desire to be a Székely woman and in no way wanted to look like an outsider or guest. Whenever we visited friends, we would be in the kitchen learning and helping cook.

We enjoyed experimenting with cooking and learnt to make mayonnaise from scratch, peanut butter, yoghurt and lemon curd. In the summer, we learnt from Bodrogi Kati how to make a refreshing elderflower drink, and I perfected the art of a delicious lemon sorbet which was never in the freezer for very long on the forty-five-degree summer days!

One memory we will never forget is the yearly pig killing. Kneeling on a pig that is slowly dying, is not in the usual experiences of a 14-year-old. Eating brain soup for lunch made from the pig you've just killed is not usual either. This was our greatest home school biology lesson of the year as we watched the pig being cut up and dissected. We learnt how big the lungs are, identified the valves in the heart, and discovered how smelly and long the intestines are as we cleaned them out to make sausages.

The Székely people taught us how to love life and how easy it is to make it great fun. I have many wonderful memories of picnicking and barbequing with the Bodrogi's on the side of roads or by forest. A whole day event including mushroom picking, swimming in the river, going exploring, singing, gypsy dancing, playing games, preparing potatoes and meat, collecting wood and cooking. I loved living in a culture where the only thing time is important for is relationships. People are prioritised. Everyone is part of a community.

We learnt how to home school in our bedroom. I think we laughed more than we learnt. Mum had to put up a curtain between us to stop us from distracting each other. However, this didn't make much of a difference; she would often return to our room to find I had given Abi a new hairstyle with chopsticks or we were rolling around laughing having found a new Chinese word that sounded like a bad word! Rach was assigned as our P.E. teacher, which, depending on the season, consisted of playing volleyball in the courtyard or sledging down the hills over the back of our garden across the frozen river and up the other hill. Who wouldn't want to go sledging for their P.E. lesson?

For five months of the year, we had to learn how to walk on ice – but, we didn't really ever learn. It was a regular occurrence falling over and bruising some part of the body, or for Mum, breaking her coccyx. We were always afraid to be the one to hold Dad up as we walked because he was notorious for not only sliding everywhere but bringing us with him, usually ending up horizontal. We did, however, learn to not freeze outside in -35°C, which was quite an art. Applying the Vaseline was vital to build a layer of fat over our skin, then we would begin the layering. By the time we got the fifth pair of socks, the third pair of trousers, the sixth t-shirt and third jumper on, it was hard to move without looking like a snowman. We found it difficult to write our schoolwork with two pairs of gloves on so we would have extra P.E. lessons to warm ourselves up! There was definitely no crying to be done outside, otherwise your eyelashes would freeze together with the water!

God taught me many things through these years as I grew up. One of the biggest lessons he taught me was about home. I remember times of wishing I belonged more to this place, and had a greater understanding of the language and culture. There were even times when I wished I was one of the kids from the orphanage so I could be an insider and understand them better. The couple of times we went home to the U.K, it was strange to feel like an outsider in my own culture and country. I dreamed of a new country, one that was not England or Romania, but home. I would feel the comfort and security of belonging in that place, and I would cry out to my Father God for this place to be real. One time this dream began again, and suddenly God spoke to me. He told me that this place is real, it's home, and while I wait for heaven, I can be at home in him. What a precious treasure of truth to learn at such a young age. It is a truth I have needed to hold onto as I continue to travel and live in different cultures.

Through my hundreds of brothers and sisters, I learnt many things. I learnt to play volleyball and attempted to breakdance; they taught me to get sunflower seeds out of the shells using only my tongue. They taught me to love even when I don't want to, and they showed me what unconditional love was. When life had been cruel and they had been rejected, abandoned and abused, they continued to survive and hold their heads up.

I have discovered that part of the identity and calling God has on my life is found in my name, Rebekah - to bind. This was my first taste of how God had called me to bind up the broken-hearted as it says in Isaiah 61. I began experiencing how God could use me to bring his healing in their lives by just being me, by loving them and accepting them for who they are. In return, my brothers and sisters enriched my life with their love in a way that is beyond words. They gave me so much just by being in my life and allowing me to be their sister.

Being family is and will always be part of my DNA, a calling on my life. Wherever I am, I naturally strive to create family and be family for those who have never experienced family love. I long to display to them what it means to know and feel the comfort, the unconditional love, the joys of living as family. This, I believe, is a natural gifting I have inherited from my parents. My parents are best at, creating, being and living *family*.

Moving back to England was pretty tough. It was two years of never fitting in, having no church to receive us back and be part of, there was a lack of community and Mum and Dad were burnt out and drained. What was the purpose of life back here? Life seemed boring and lonely. Mum and Dad needed a period of recovery, and there was not much help available or time for them to do this. They had to get back into full time work quickly as we had no money left and didn't have time to process the last three years. This had a big effect on me, and I didn't understand their change of heart/calling as I saw it through my teenage eyes. I didn't understand why for a time they closed down and no longer wanted to welcome others into our home and our family, when this is what 'we did'. Now as an adult in a similar situation, I realise what happens emotionally when you have an open home for years, where you continually give and don't have much input – your heart becomes tired and your capacity to welcome is reduced. I now wonder how my parents actually survived and adjusted to life back in Surrey. They did their best in the circumstances they were in. I went back to the same school for my A-levels, and the group of friends I had before I left for Romania had changed and grown closer. I didn't understand the things they talked about, the experiences they had had or the values they clung to. Through these two years, God reminded me again of how to feel at home in Him and not in a place or among a people. I didn't need to strive to fit in, but to be at home in Him and find my belonging in my identity as His child.

Romania and the Székely people will always have a precious place in my heart. I am blessed and privileged to have lived amongst these people and to have journeyed this adventure with my family and God.

Here is my record of a journey from Székelyudvarhely (Udvarhely) to Székelykeresztúr(Keresztúr) and then onto Brașov.

REVELATIONS OF GOD THROUGH A JOURNEY IN A VALLEY CALLED HOME

This is awe-inspiring driving through the valley we call home between Udvarhely and Keresztúr,

The green fields and hills sunlit with your favour Lord,

The indescribable brightness of the village houses reflecting your happiness and joy in life,

These bloomin' potholes that eventually become my comfort,

It reminds me of how you release a deep peace within us in the difficult times when we are shaken up,

The frost covering this sunny morning bringing your spiritual cleansing and refreshment for the people to embrace as they awake,

The atmosphere of splendour and beauty in nothing but the hills and villages and even in the chaos of the poverty and worn out crumbling buildings,

Within all this is a sense of home and indescribable beauty,

You are amongst the everyday happenings, your beauty can still shine through though there be pain,

The crippled old ladies who look worn out and overworked,

And yet they still manage a smile as they natter to the neighbour outside their village houses waiting for the cows to find their way home from the hills,

Their engraved faces tell of the horror and cruelty of the past,

But their smiles tell of the strength and endurance you have given them,

The sun browned men walking out to their fields for a long day's work with their spade swung over their shoulder,

As we cross the bridge it feels as though it were soon to give way yet it feels safe as it seems almost built into nature,

The iron railway running alongside the river like something out of 'the railway children', I watch children running along it missing every other plank and it reminds me to have faith like a child enjoying your blessings and the fun and freedom you give,

The meandering river glistening from the kiss of the sun,

The gypsies washing their clothes in the murky water where the horses are also having a bath, I wonder to myself if the clothes were cleaner before they were washed,

The approaching scene of each village from the road as little pockets of buildings with the familiar bright white steeple standing taller than all the other buildings as the centre piece of this picture proclaiming you are at the centre of us, you are amongst us and yet you are the highest and greatest,

We are embraced by the mist lingering in the valley that is hovering over the hills and houses, whilst the sun's rays shine through reflecting your mystery,

And yet in this you reveal to us aspects of who you are and your will becomes piercingly clear,

Slowly approaching the jagged snow-capped mountains surrounding Brașov all lined up to provoke inspiration, and to sing out your magnificence to all whose eyes they capture.

THE ROAD TO TRANSYLVANIA

CHAPTER 24

ABI

My first memory is of us all sitting in our living room in Cobham hearing about Anne and Dad's recent trip to Romania. They were so excited and full of energy that the rest of us felt exhausted hearing all they had done. The next words that Dad said would change not just the way that I grew up, but my understanding of learning and fitting into another culture.

Just the idea of moving to Romania was a bit daunting, but I was filled with not only a sense of peace but also adventure and excitement. The first challenge that we were set was to go away and pray and then regroup and chat about what God had shown or spoken to us. Becky's picture stuck out to me; it was of a hot air balloon that was overflowing with

ABI

money. One of my parents' concerns was how we were going to support ourselves whilst living in Romania, as we were heading as volunteers. This was God's way of showing us that He would provide what we needed.

I was at the age that most children go through about wanting a dog, and Mum and Dad always came up with a reason why we couldn't. So, as I was praying, I asked God to change their minds and allow me to have a dog when we moved. God answered this prayer as when I brought up the topic they agreed straight away. The story of our miracle puppy is in Chapter 6. No matter how big or small my wants or wishes were, God really showed me that he cared for every minor detail in my life.

The next step in our journey was to go on a summer camp that was run every year for the children from the orphanage. The aim of us joining the team was for us to experience life in Romania and see if we liked it. I thoroughly enjoyed the experience and loved being on the camp, sitting around campfires, playing games and testing out the Romanian food. I instantly knew that Romania was the place that God wanted us to be family to the orphans. Unbeknown to us girls, this would then lead to us learning to share our parents with around 200 young people and accepting them as our brothers and sisters. The grace and understanding that God equipped us with allowed us to enjoy and make the most of our extending family. I loved the feeling and atmosphere when they were around - we were family. After we returned, we decided as a family to follow this calling to Romania.

On leaving England, we were only allowed to take one suitcase and box with us and leave one box of belongings behind. Asking an 11-year-old to sort through all possessions and pack the necessary was quite challenging, but I managed it. We packed our VW minibus and started our journey across to Romania, travelling through France, Belgium, Netherlands, Germany, Austria, Hungary and finally reaching Romania on the fourth day. As we would discover over the next three years, these journeys would provide not only a sense of adventure but also how to get on as a family, and we learnt so much about each other. This is one of the reasons why we sisters are so close. We invented numerous games, experienced different cultures, tested out youth hostels and invented ways to keep the minivan cool in the hot summers.

We arrived in Romania and moved into our house that Mum had organised on a previous visit. It was opposite a cattle market which happened every Tuesday morning where you would be woken up by the sound of cows at 5 am. It was such an experience to watch the commotion, so I used to sit on our fence at the front whilst eating cherries off the cherry tree. From observing this for three years I learnt the art of selling a cow Romanian style. Our garden was on a slope as it backed onto the hills and mountains behind, and yes, there were bears living in the forests behind our house. We never saw any but we saw the evidence whilst dog walking one day, and we got told off by our neighbours for walking when it was getting dark as that is when the bears come down and on the path was proof that a bear had been along very recently. This new culture was the start of a new way of living, cooking from scratch as no ready meals, collecting milk from the milk lady and having to boil it and having to collect water from the local spring as you couldn't drink the tap water.

So, our adventure began.

Becky and I were home schooled through an organisation based in England, but our classmates were living in different countries around the world. I really enjoyed having school in our bedroom. Although I'm not sure how Bex and I ever got any work done, we were good at distracting each other. We were sent our work at the beginning of the week which we had to complete and send back to our tutors by the end of the week. This made it flexible, so I used to work really hard for the first three days and then have the rest of the week off so I could join Dad when he had to go places. Having been home schooled it taught me a lot, for example, time management, responsibility and how to learn through practical means. I grew up a lot faster than I would have back in the UK, having started secondary school. I am so thankful for this as my eyes were opened to the ways of the world at a young age and would determine how I lived my life.

God answered one of my key prayers. The puppy was only the size of my hand, and we had many adventures; I called him Barney. There was an incident where on a walk he had somehow got himself stuck on a ledge on the end of a steep drop. We had to call our neighbour to help us, as we had to throw ropes down so we could climb down and get him. Another time we were collecting water from the spring as we did every week and above the spring is a steep slope. As my Dad was filling up the bottles, Becky and I decided to climb the zig-zag path up the slope which was a bit muddy. However, on the way down I slipped, and as I was about to fall off the side of the path down the hill, I felt someone grab my sleeve stopping me falling off the edge. I turned around to find it was Barney, my dog who had grabbed my arm. He was a clever dog who would always be beside you, was fearless and always looked out for you. In a way, he reminded me of God as he is always there watching over us and protecting us. God had provided me with a faithful and servant-hearted dog. One of the hardest things for me was not being able to bring him back with us when we moved back to England - it was very difficult at that time and he would have had to go into quarantine for six months which he would not have coped with. However, another miracle was the week before we left Romania, the school down the road had just lost their guard dog due to old age. We knew one of the teachers who worked there, and she talked to the director who agreed for Barney to become their new guard dog. This made it easier for me to leave him, as I knew he would be looked after well.

One of my responsibilities was to collect the milk every other morning from one of our neighbours. If I got up early enough, I would help her with the milking which was done all by hand. She was abundant in her generosity and always asked me in for a drink and biscuits to say thank you. This added to my love for animals and contributed to who I am now.

Life in Romania was very different from England. Horse and cart or walking were the main modes of transport. There were very few cars on the roads. Hungarian is meant to be one of the hardest languages after the picture languages, which seemed very daunting when we first moved, as we didn't understand anything. Being young, it meant it came quite freely to me and I loved the challenge of learning the language. By the end of the three years, I was nearly fluent. Mice were a big problem in Romania, especially in the winter; they particularly enjoyed eating our English chocolate that we were saving that people had bought over for us.

The winters in Romania were stunning and provided much entertainment. For around four to five months of the year, we had snow and ice. Rachel and I used to skate along while the others were trying to hold each other up. We used to go sledging on the hills behind our house and in our garden, which ended up with Paul almost losing his nose as he went under the fence into our allotment.

Every Sunday, we opened our house up to the young people to join us in worship, eating and sharing encouraging words. I never knew how far food could stretch. We catered for about thirty to forty people and often around fifty to sixty would turn up, yet the food was still enough. It reminded us of feeding the five thousand in the Bible - only God could have made this possible.

I thoroughly enjoyed our time in Romania, learning the language, spending time with the young people from the children's home, living in a different culture and seeing how God works through mysterious ways. From this I learnt that God often uses animals to show me His faithfulness and that He cares about me. He strengthened my faith during these years and showed me that He was there no matter how big or small our worries and concerns. Over the three years our family expanded by a large number, but with God's grace and protection, we grew in faith and were stronger together.

CHAPTER 25

SZTOIKA CSABA

At the beginning of my part, I want to say thank you to Phil Slade for giving me the chance to write in his book. I have known him since my childhood, and he is like my own Father. We first met in April 1998 at a camp. Often, we laugh about our first meeting, where we played chess, and I beat him.

My name is Sztoika Csaba; born, grew up in Romania, and since 2010 I have lived in Germany. I have always wanted to help people who need help. Old or young, strong or weak, rich or poor, in families or orphans.

SZTOIKA CSABA

Phil and Elaine lived in Romania for three years. When Phil felt it was time for his family to return to England, he started a Social Action business working with village craft people. He asked me to help him with translation and for two years, I participated in helping him with the practical and financial details in Romania. I helped him with his work with Heart for Romania and helped him with lots of negotiations. After two years, I went on to work and travel in Europe in places like San Marino, Switzerland, France and Germany. I have learned and experienced many new things like languages, cultures and different mentalities about life.

After some years, I decided that I wanted to stay in Germany and have lived there since 2010. I contacted Phil, and the idea of working in a business partnership became a reality as we put together a business idea of Craft Uk & Sztoika+Enterprise. In early 2015, we decided that we would work together. I would take over the business concept and bring new input.

In 2015, between Christmas and New Year I had the idea to build a new innovative product - Qime Life Is More Solar Wireless Charging Pad. This product re-imagines intelligent furniture, and I hope this will be a new trend on the Global Markets. I have now started my own Start-Up Businesses, Sztoika +Enterprise, and one new Start-Up, Qime Company's. It was always my wish to be a good Christian entrepreneur, and now I have a chance from God. I really want to thank Phil for praying for me and for mentoring me as I started my road to business. Matthias Braun also mentored and encouraged me.

This book, about the journey of the Slade family life, which was incredible, shows the world what can be achieved. Maybe Phil will do some new projects and I am sure God will support him. I pray for this!

Consider it pure joy, my brothers and sisters, whenever you face trials of many kinds.

James 1:12

CHAPTER 26

PAUL KNOWLSON

Meeting the Slade family.

I had the pleasure of first meeting the Slade family at the first church I attended, Pioneer People back in 1997 when I was 26 years old. Back then, I had the opportunity of working and serving under Phil and Elaine's leadership and volunteering for a kid's club, called Buzz, which in essence was a gospel presentation for kids run by kids. I still remember those planning meetings, sitting on the living room floor among around twenty people, including both kids and teenagers and just remarking on the Slade family's joy, kindness and serving hearts beaming out in all that they were doing. I also remember having to wear the oversized 'Hale and Pace' style Buzz hat and t-shirt, and jumping around everywhere in a school hall thinking, "God, what on earth am I doing here?" I think this just summed up Phil and Elaine; you would do anything for them because first they were doing it - and loving it!

Out of my experience of Buzz I started to get to know the Slade family, and at that time sooner or later the conversation would be drawn to Romania. Then in late 1998 early 1999, I was asked if I would consider joining them on the summer camp mission. I still remember having a conversation with Phil and Elaine about it. I didn't have an issue of going per-se; I was in employment and could easily take annual leave, so money and time wasn't an issue. I was more concerned about what I could add or do, as I didn't really feel a heart for Romania. If I was honest, I didn't really have a heart or gifting for youth or kids work, I was doing Buzz just trying to be obedient and to serve.

I loved and still really appreciate their response, "Paul don't worry about what you are going to do, God knows and will show you, and anyway we know you'll be a support to us as a family, as a team." Personally, this is almost the DNA of the Slades; assuring you and inviting you to be part of their family. Well, that just took all pressure off and I guess dissolved any pre-conceived ideas I had.

The planning meetings were so encouraging, yet simple and joyful. As part of our team we had two early teens with us, no real church background, no Christian decision (I believe), straight out of an Alpha course! Phil and Elaine always seemed to honour people's heart, always had room to include, and encourage.

Anyway, back to Romania summer camp, and of course Phil and Elaine were quite right about God showing me how, what and who to serve. It was obvious; just watch what the Slade family where doing, rolling their sleeves up, getting stuck in and just loving all these children, in a Christ-like manner. Looking back, you could see the genuine love, passion and heart for those children, that people group, the area and the country. It was no surprise when I learned of God's plans for them all. I learnt so much during those two weeks in Romania, and what now seems like quite an adventure. For instance, hob-nob biscuits and cereal bars had more commodity value than English pounds and passports!

Then there was the simple appreciation of running water, soup consisting of more than a chicken's claw and water and lard sandwiches! However, and more importantly, those two weeks did change my life. Without sounding dramatic, my outlook, attitudes, and my untapped desire had been ignited by seeing the Slade's kindness, passion and heart for those children. God had flamed in me a greater passion to serve Him, to be as Jesus to the people, showing His power and unconditional and relentless love, just like I saw the Slade family living out.

Joining the Slade family in Romania.

I was still working for a large international electronic equipment company, travelling in Europe but was deeply unsatisfied. Inside, I still carried a passion to serve God in a greater way from the experience in Romania. In May 2003, I sensed the Lord releasing me from my employment, so there and then I handed in my resignation and knew this was the season to pursue His will fully. I also sensed the Lord saying that I had too many safety nets to really follow and trust Him; with the safety nets representing possessions. So, I pretty much relinquished everything I had.

That was a really exciting time and looking back, I can see the jigsaw of God's will and provision for my life. I spent three months in the United States with my very good friends, the Gemmells. It was there they suggested attending Co-Mission, a missionary training and equipping course. Back in the UK, in October 2003, I attend this course led by Linda Harding in Llanelli, South Wales. After the course, whilst speaking to Linda, I explained that I had a heart to serve God and wanted to go on Mission. I remember praying at that time asking God not to send me to two countries, Romania being one of them - I wanted to experience a new culture. So, when Linda suggested approaching the Slades on the possibility in joining them I thought, typical; that is God's sense of humour, be careful what you pray!

After initial talks with Phil and Elaine and members of Heart for Romania, who were so supportive, it was agreed that I would fly out to Romania on January 14th, 2004. Initially, the idea was to look at the possibility of me living in shared accommodation, possibly with some of the young indigenous adults. However, after discussions, it was agreed I would stay with the Slades and increase the male population of the household. Yet again, I experienced another example of who the Slades are, and yet again, I was encouraged and invited to be part of their family.

Although it was only six months, it was six months full of twenty-four hour a day rich teaching, modelling, discipleship and life applying demonstrations of faith, love and power in action, in other words, church. I honestly believe I would not have gained this amazing example anywhere else or with anyone else. God is amazing and it's amazing to see God through His people.

During those six months I can recount a number of answered prayers and numerous accounts of His miraculous provision. Our *feeding of the five thousand with five loaves and two fish* occasions were often feeding the additional ten hungry teenagers at the table with half a bag of rice, packet of mince and a near-empty pot of mustard. I remember the instances of God being with me during many times of feeling out of my depth and completely lost within a culture that held a belief system that was just confusing. God's peace and favour was always present during those times of bewildered or when I was in tears seeing such social deprivation and injustice which hit to the core the poorest of the poor. I witnessed God's Kingdom unfold before my eyes through the action of a family with great faith and a huge heart.

I feel obliged to say that the most impacting element, the most valuable experience God gave me during my time in Romania, is the ministry of the Slade family. To this day, their influence is instilled in me and is benefitting my current ministry as a Pastor. I believe that 'simple faith' takes ground. There are a few Christians who are more interested in denominational differences, needing theological debates, and where being correct is too important. The marginalised are interested in reality because they live in reality, not debate rooms. They're interested in motivation, genuineness and action - this is where the Slade family excel and excel as a family. We can all get caught up with numeric success, numeric growth as opposed to growth in individual's lives and the success of a heart and passion for seeing God move in a community, people group or geographic area. The Slades were only interested in the latter; they were too concerned for the individual and willing them to encounter the Jesus that they themselves knew, followed and loved.

They would welcome all and everyone, not to an event but to be part of them, as a family in a real, open and, trusting relationship. I believe God called them to be family to the whole community. I still remember how the girls were streets ahead of me in connecting with the young teenagers we worked with. They all seemed to be relentless in their capacity to reach out to these orphaned teenagers and had the ability to 'thaw' the hard protection mechanism that many of the teenagers had developed.

Looking back the cost the whole family were willing to pay, and in some cases paid, was amazing, particularly Phil and

Elaine, being parents. However, they never seemed to doubt the goodness of God and His wiliness to bless them.

Finally, I've learnt the importance of having around you *people of peace*, and the Slades had been blessed by these – the amazing Bodrogi Csaba.

I doubt if the Slades will ever get the accolades, the awards or even the recognition they deserve, yet I'm sure they wouldn't want them. Knowing all of this family, they will value the treasures they are storing up in heaven.

CHAPTER 27

BODROGI CSABA

Szekely Land, or how locals say, "Székelyföld," is on the map of Romania, part of Transylvania, where a Hungarian speaking community live. People of this region are continuing a daily fight to keep their language and culture, to be able to leave the heritage of more than 1100 years for coming generations. Protecting the Hungarian language for many is a way to keep going and survive in the midst of another language speaking majority.

When I begin to speak about my 50 years of life, I start with a word, Mother. In Hungarian; Anya. Love and affection showed by these women is reflected in how most of Seclers would say to their mother Édesanya (which means, Sweet Mother). I can remember when I was a child, if somebody said "Anya," I always argued with them and said, "I have no Mother, I have a Sweet Mother. Such was the way I addressed the person who gave me life, raised me and protected my brothers and me too.

For an 8-year-old child, at the beginning of the 70s, they were confusing times. The regime and the school did not recognise God, but many of the families tried to educate their children in the spirit of the Loving Father. My beloved Father took my hand, and at Sundays, we went to the Reformat Church from the centre of the town.

Something happened at a service that I did not understand until many, many years after. The Priest said, "You must love God even better than your mother." I thought, "No way, this is an offence, it is impossible, I cannot love anybody more than my Sweet Mother. I do not understand what is in the Priest's mind!" Years passed away quickly, the usual things that happen in a man's life occurred; studies, Army, job, family, children. Some bad things, some good things. I became a young man who was doing well; a loving father, successful in his job, respected by others, but something was missing.

Sometime during July 1997, on a hot summer's afternoon, I invited a new colleague of mine to have a cold beer. We started socialising, talking about the coming opportunities, in the friendly environment of the Vadrozsa Hotel. After a couple of minutes, the owner of the place, named Lajos, introduced a man to me. He was obviously a foreigner, he didn't speak Hungarian or Romanian, but he had a special appearance and smile. We greeted each other, and with my modest English language skills we opened a new chapter in our lives. The feeling was that he seemed familiar to me, like I had known him for a long time. He was Phil, Philip W. Slade. We both know now that this meeting was arranged for us by God Himself.

After a couple of beers our two families sat together at one table in my house, ten persons, Phil and Elaine, his wonderful wife, their lovely four daughters, my wife Kati, our son Lehel, and our daughter Kincsö. We have shared many meals since then, and we have had so many quality times together. 'Friendship' became a deeper meaning for us; it took on a superior dimension.

During the time they were living in Odorheiu Secuiesc I learned a lot from Phil, and I tried to help them live their experience here. Pig killings (keep calm, the circumstances were legal), visiting other villages, towns, people and so on. But the most wonderful thing we have ever done was when we prayed together. The way Phil prays, with closed eyes and taking our hands was different from the way we used to pray before. God was there, present, with us.

I remember very well the evening when I told Phil & Elaine that I was living a good and respectable life, but felt something was missing. Elaine responded, "Csaba, you are doing well, but from now on do everything with Jesus, Go everywhere with Jesus."

Phil and Elaine are part of our lives, an example of how to organise, live and love. We are very proud of their work, and we are amazed by what they accomplished by trusting and loving the Lord. Dozens of young people address them as Mum & Father. I am convinced that God sent Phil and his family to us just to show us something even better - His love.

I have now lived through the most successful phase of my life. If I analyse my 50 years, I can say I had bad and good periods, but in every situation, my family and my friends were with me. However, one thing became very clear to me; when I faced problems, it would be very difficult without Jesus to solve them. Everything I've done is because He, the Lord, loves me and leads me. When nothing is going as I would wish, in my frailty, I ask the Lord what to do and how to do it. As Phil said, "He is the jam in our sandwich." The Light of the world.

I now understand the Priest from the Reform Church, both with my mind and heart. Yes, it is possible and even better to love God more than anybody. If you love God, you are at peace with yourself. His love is the never-ending spring. Thank you, Phil & Elaine, for helping me understand it.

*A friend loves at all times,
and a brother is born for a time of adversity.'*

Proverbs 17: 17

CHAPTER 28

FAZAKAS ISTVÁN (PISTI)

The situation of the Children's Homes in 1990 was well known; we saw so many reports and shocking pictures which revealed the inhumanities and atrocity of the communist regime. In Kerestúr/Cristuru Secuiesc was the biggest Children's Home. Before 1989, this institution had 650 children. During this time, the State made sure there was a place to live and work after the children left. After 1990, there was no provision.

To resolve this situation, the people who worked in the institution and some German Christian people came with some relief supplies. They set up an association to aid the youngsters moving on from the Children's home. The activity of the Domus charity (Domus Association) was a pioneering one. A lot of problems were resolved with the help of good-willed people. In a few years, we were able to buy apartments and to build a family house for the young people. We also looked for employment for the young people. This is how we made connections with a lot of good-hearted foreign people.

Sometime after 2000, I heard that there was an English family in Udvarhely who had a connection with the Domus Association. Soon I made a visit with Dorit to Udvarhely, and we met the Slade family. I have to say that our overseas sponsors were mainly Germans and we were already accustomed to them, and the relationship with the English charity started slowly because of the language barrier. Even so, there was an immediate empathy which grew quickly with Phil, Elaine and their daughters. From the first moment, it was obvious that the Romanian teenagers from the Domus Association felt welcome in the English family's house and they were often there.

A joint work started, in the first instance to help the young people in Udvarhely. A very good working method formed between Phil, Dorit and myself. We would meet every Monday morning at Phil's house and drink English tea with milk and decide the week's to-do list. I wasn't accustomed to drinking milk with tea; milk is milk and tea is tea, we don't mix the two! But this was how we got used to English tea. The Monday meetings proved to be very effective, and it later became a tradition to meet with the whole work community on Monday. Today this is how we now start the week in our organisation.

When you are working with somebody, you get to know that person better and you develop feelings for them. After a short while, I realised that Phil and his family were very open-hearted people. They accommodated young people and their home became a place for their common activities. It is beautiful to see a harmonious family; this was an attractive example, often twenty or more youngsters were in their home. For this, of course, it was necessary in the first place to have a motherly figure such as Elaine. She not only soothed their physical hunger but resolved a lot of their other problems too.

It was surprising how quickly Phil managed to fit into the life of the town, building relationships which he used to help the young people. There were a few situations which were hard to manage even with joint forces; difficulties with the rented apartments of the English organisation. But it is only after all these years I can appreciate Phil's attitude, patience and approach. Owing to that, a lot of youngsters became independent and are now abroad and, often incidentally, are in England.

I am happy that our relationship is strong even now. Our families became firm friends, we have met repeatedly over the years, and this is how we find out how the youngsters are getting on in England.

> *But the Lord said to Samuel, "Do not consider his appearance or his height, for I have rejected him. The Lord does not look at the things people look at. People look at the outward appearance, but the Lord looks at the heart."*
>
> *1 Samuel 16:7*

This was said several times and helped us in our work, but I would rather say that this is the feeling that developed in our hearts regarding Phil and his family because they saw our hearts too. The beating of their English hearts here in Romania wasn't just a family adventure or a trip. Their hearts were beating so resoundingly, that it gave the young people confidence in their life paths towards independence.

THE ROAD TO TRANSYLVANIA

CHAPTER 29

BODROGI LEHEL

"The future of humanity depends on people who are based on truth, and whose lives are permeated with high moral principles, whose heart enables the self-sacrifice of enduring love."

John Paul II: Thoughts About Life

The quote from John Paul II sums up the character of the Slade family. I am Bodrogi Csaba's son. I could never say it was a chance encounter, our 17-year long relationship and friendship. Even as a child, I knew that this growing friendship was based on common sympathy. It was exciting when the phone rang and I would hear my father greeting, "Hi Phil, how are you?" After the chat, my sister and I always asked our father about the conversation. It felt such an amazing thing to know that the Slades were calling from England to enquire about us. On holidays or birthdays, we received a card from England, most of the time to thank us for our hospitality.

Soon they decided to move to Romania so they could help the orphan children through the charity Heart for Romania. They were interested in helping the Székelykeresztúr Children's Home, which was functioning with inadequate governmental support. Several times I went to Szekelykeresztur to experience the conditions the children lived in and learned to be thankful to have such a wonderful family. If only the children there could have had the same. It was a life-changing experience to be able to go to the Sos Kut camp and to see how they managed to put a smile on the children's faces. I learned a lot myself. I enjoyed the activities, especially with the different paints I could colour my own shirt. Thinking back, I realise that everybody painted their shirt about the friendship or friend that they had made during the camp.

In their home which was almost full all the time, affection was felt in a different way. Everybody was chilled, some of them playing football in the courtyard, whilst others helped with the cooking or braided each other's hair. After these activities there was always time for joint praying, followed by music and songs. I can hear even now the guitar and the young people's voices. This was the mood and what can be more fulfilling than when the Slade parents were called mum and dad by the many children.

Time went by and the children became grownups, many finished university. Almost everybody spoke English and with a little help, many of them are working in England or other countries. Some have their own families now. When I visited England, a grown-up Kereszturen orphan served me in a restaurant, and another guided me through London's tourist sites.

Finally, I'd like to thank the Slades for the opportunity to write a few lines. I can't wait to see the book.

CHAPTER 30

TIM POOLE

Romanian dictator Nicolae Ceauşescu and his wife, Elena, were tried and executed on Christmas Day 1989. British newspapers were soon full of horrendous pictures of babies and children in many Romanian children's homes, suffering severe neglect, and lack of nourishment and affection. Groups from all over Europe were moved to send in help in the form of clothing, food, medicines, materials for repairs and above all, a great compassion for those suffering from Ceauşescu's regime.

Our small church in Cobham, Surrey, formed one of those groups. Told about a huge Children's Home in the middle of Transylvania, a group of about a dozen men packed vans with clothing, building materials, cans of diesel fuel, and oranges, the latter generously donated by the local Primary School. They set off across Europe into the seemingly unknown. Arriving in the small town of Cristuru Secuiesc which housed the largest Children's Home in the county of Harghita with six hundred and fifty, they discovered that their Romanian phrasebooks brought with them were of no use as they were in the middle of the Hungarian-speaking part of Romania. Transylvania was of course once part of the Austro-Hungarian Empire, until

Hungary was forced to cede the area after being on the wrong side in both World Wars.

Language, however, is not an impenetrable barrier to communication, and so the group, housed in the Home itself, set to making friends, repairing whatever and wherever possible and planning for the future. This was the birth of what was then called Cobham Romania Aid. The Deputy Director of the Home, Bernád Rozi, was beginning to learn English and became a firm friend and has been so for the past twenty-five years. In 1991, I was invited to join the second team to visit the Home with the task of totally renovating the girls' shower and washrooms. Not being gifted in DIY, I was soon released by the team to go and build friendships with the young people of the home. Such friendships have lasted now over a quarter of a century, and it is encouraging to see how so many young people have succeeded in life after such difficult early years.

Success was not always the outcome for the young people who, at the age of 18 were forced to leave the Home and make their way in life with no family, no job, no money and no home. Some ended up in criminal activities and some in prostitution. A local organisation known as Domus tried to help many of them with accommodation, and this was successful in varying degrees. Many of the youngsters wanted to leave the town, with its memories, and start life anew. I opened a flat in the larger neighbouring town of Odorheiu Secuiesc, providing accommodation in a town where employment opportunities were more readily available, and the stigma of being brought up in a Home was no longer a problem.

Meanwhile, work in the Children's Home developed in the form of summer camps. Teenagers from the church in Cobham were invited to work with young Romanian children in the beautiful setting of the Transylvanian countryside. Friendships were made which are still flourishing, and the young Cobham people came home with a very different perspective on life, many determined to keep going back year on year. A key part of the camps was the sharing of faith. Bilingual Bibles were purchased - studies and prayer were regular features. We saw God work in many situations.

The Fatherhood of God was a difficult concept for those who had no experience of being fathered. Times of great emotion and plenty of tears were had around huge campfires, where dramas were performed to illustrate God's love and care for each one. Prayers were said in English and Hungarian with the Holy Spirit clearly interpreting their meaning.

As part of joining the European Union, Romania was encouraged to close their huge, impersonal institutions. Those children who were still under the care of the state were subsequently housed in flats and houses; some purchased privately by charities and churches and some financed by grants from the EU. The benefits experienced by the youngsters were regular home-cooked meals, clean clothes and greater privacy, but many were disappointed to be separated from their friends from the larger institution. The closing of the Children's Home, which subsequently became a Technology College, meant that the camps were not so easy to organise.

Cobham Romania Aid soon became a charity in its own right and took the name Heart for Romania. The small group of workers involved felt that God was encouraging us to work with the poorest section of the community – the Roma, or gypsies. Although some of the Romanian gypsy population have considerable wealth, there are many living in slum-like conditions. There is abject poverty and often a spirit of depression and despair in these communities. The small village that we chose to work with, only five minutes away from the town of Cristuru Secuiesc, was home to about thirty families and a seemingly endless number of children. Many of the villagers had been brought up in the Children's Home that we and been working in, and so on our first visit it seemed that a number of them remembered us. This was a useful entrée.

We discovered that employment was often very hard to find for both the men and the women of the village. They had very few qualifications, and many were unable to read or write. On occasions, this would lead to a certain apathy amongst the menfolk who could tend to give up hope of work. Many however would travel to Hungary in certain seasons and find agricultural work, often leaving their children in the village to be cared for by others.

The homes were tiny with no foundations, had mud flooring and were open to all the vagaries of the weather. Snow and rain came plentifully into almost every home, creating an unhealthy environment for the many children. Two of us decided to speak with the villagers and gather from them how they felt we could help. We wanted to bless them and support them, but at the same time not impose our own ideas and culture. They said they were desperate for help with their housing – something that was clearly obvious to us on our first visit.

We also noticed that the only supply of water came from a small well which, because the sanitation facilities in the village were non-existent, produced only fetid water. Discussions with the local mayor led to water pipes being laid to each house, providing fresh water to homes for the first time. Mothers could now wash their clothes, children and food. They were very happy! A young man, András, who himself was brought up in the Children's Home, had built his own house in a different village where he had married a local girl and was happy to use his skills to rebuild or repair the homes in the village. Currently, we have rebuilt or repaired about twenty homes. A home is one room of five square metres, but with a concrete floor and a weatherproof roof.

We spent some time visiting the local Primary School in the village. On roll were thirty-six gypsy children. Non-gypsies did not attend, preferring to go to the school in the town. An average daily attendance seemed to be about twelve. Without a school diploma and basic reading, writing and maths skills, chances of finding employment were poor. We set about encouraging the mothers to send their children to school. Often the excuse was they had no shoes. This was easily remedied by sending out shoes from England and frequenting the town's shoe shop. However, this did not always remedy the absence from school.

Now the work continues, with good relationships being made and various teams coming from the UK to encourage and to support, with the hope of the villagers becoming self-sustained. The gypsies feel discriminated against, and the town's people take offence to their lack of cleanliness and sometimes their dishonesty. It seems that our role is to try to bring two such communities together for their mutual benefit, as well as maintaining the warm relationships we have built with so many families.

THE ROAD TO TRANSYLVANIA

CHAPTER 31

THINGS WE HAVE LEARNT

When God gives you a passion for something, don't give up until He closes the door. Very much like a covered passage, it may be dark ahead and you may have to fight through cobwebs, but as you step into what He has to offer, the light comes on and if you look back, it's now dark behind. That's all right. It's how it has to be. Yes, we need those memories but don't step back.

If you are going for something which involves the whole family, make sure it does involve the whole family. Get their perspectives at the beginning. Get them to pray it through and if they are young, get them to pray it through with someone else you and they trust. Then get their perspective on it again.

If you are going into a risky plan, having got the support and advice from those you know and trust, get some independent advice from someone who does not know you but who has a trusted track record. We were very fortunate to be interviewed as a family and individuals by Pat Cook, who was brought in by Pioneer People to test our calling. It confirmed both for the senders and ourselves that this was what God was calling us into. Also, you have got someone else who is accountable for your decision!

Listen to your children, no matter how young they are. God spoke to David in the bible as a young boy. He spoke to our Becky as a young girl about telling people about Jesus, and He spoke to the other girls. They very often hear God plainly without all the baggage we often have. Show that you take them seriously.

Don't do something because of people's expectations if God has not told you to especially if it takes you away from the first calling. Had we taken through and led Alpha ourselves in Romania, we would not have got the visit from a man a year later after introducing it, saying they were now ready to take it on themselves. It was hard at the time not to take control when we knew we could do it, but would it have been sustainable? We had to allow God to be in control. The resulting Alpha courses were very successful because they were culturally relevant.

Be prepared to learn about the new culture; don't make assumptions. We were told to make sure we had cross-cultural training which we did and then immersed ourselves in the lives of a family living in the area to understand their culture. We still got things wrong, but not as much as if we had not prepared in the way we did. The cross-cultural training included the children too and was very practical. Very important.

We must be prepared to allow ourselves to be challenged on the way we do things and why. It may not be the best way, especially in a culture which does things differently. It's great if we can learn from them. They will learn from us just in the way we say and do things. We do not go to teach and change their lives and to make them do it like us. We go to serve.

We found that the best way to introduce people to Jesus is to try to think, what would Jesus do in this situation? Praying that they see Jesus in the way we responded to situations was our goal.

We were so glad we were allowed to serve in Romania without a project title. It was The Slades in Romania. We were just there to be! What God did was through us was not through strategies or major plans but through being there living with the people on a daily basis. We were available as required.

The loosely used phrase, "He ordered it; He'll pay for it" often comforted us as the bank balance did not reflect the cash that we had. We always had more. Why I say loosely used, is that it does not mean we do not look seriously at the finance of a plan. Of course, this is wise and correct, using the financially God-given skills of others. We are glad we did. When one is however in a challenging situation, we are reminded of the verse in Philippians 4:19 that God will supply all our needs. We made sure our accounts could be audited so we could be accountable for what we were spending.

THE ROAD TO TRANSYLVANIA

THE ROAD TO TRANSYLVANIA

EPILOGUE

I guess we all feel that being able to make a difference in the life or lives of others is an aspiration we look to. Being Jesus in a daily situation is far more difficult it seems back in the UK than in a different country where we are often out of our comfort zone and living on the edge. People often say to us that we must be an extraordinary family to have done what we did, but we are ordinary people that God used in an extraordinary way. Never think you are not equipped or talented enough; all that God requires is that we say, "Yes" when He calls us.

This life in Romania prepared the girls for their adventures doing mission abroad. Anne has already told me that going through drafts of this book has inspired her to write her story on serving on the Doulos. Elaine and I have cheered the girls on from the side-lines in this particular season, although my basket business kept me travelling back and forwards across Europe to Romania which kept those links going. We certainly love being in other countries. What the future has in store none of us know. I know I want to live another adventure again. Elaine feels the same, so I guess we shall see.

A NOTE FROM ELAINE

During a trip to Operation Mobilisation's Headquarters in Shropshire, UK, when accompanying our daughter Becky on short leave from abroad in January 2016, Phil was asked by a member of staff, "What are you doing now?" This led to his next adventure in the workplace. He is now a Partner Development Manager with the OM UK team making connections mainly in the South of England between churches/organisations and OM UK. In a worldwide context, Phil focuses on the Himalayas and Europe, which has meant that he has travelled a lot, both on his own and taking teams out to visit personnel that they support from their church.

OM's focus is to seek to give everyone in the least reached people groups across the world the opportunity to hear about Jesus at least once. He has thoroughly enjoyed connecting with churches and organisations and OMers serving abroad and enabling better communication between home and field. Phil had felt that maybe that he had served his purpose by the age of 63 and there wouldn't be the prospect of a last job before retirement. God had other plans. We often remark that many of the experiences that Phil had had during his working life up to then were preparing him for this final paid position.

God led me into leadership in my Primary School; influencing others through my Early Years moderator role and helping to write both the County and Diocesan RE schemes of work. I also wrote the Early Years scheme of work for the Diocese, alongside mentoring teachers in training and newly qualified teachers. I finished my career as a Deputy Head. In all these areas, God used the experiences I had during Romania, whether they were challenges or successes. Nothing is ever wasted.

EPILOGUE

We were home from the mission field abroad, but God continued to challenge us to live on the edge and move out of our comfort zone in many different ways. Whilst Phil was getting to grips with his new job, I was sensing that my time had come to retire from teaching but what would I do next? Any doors that I tried stayed shut.

At Christmas we received a card from a lady who lived with Becky in the Himalayas which had a verse in it; Don't forget the dreams you had when you were a child. In one sense, it could have been easily overlooked, but I kept thinking about it. To be honest, I had long forgotten my own dreams, replacing them with what the family needed over the years. Asking God what it meant, I mused over the fact that I had often wanted to be a stay-at-home mum rather than full-time teacher at school, but it was too late for that to be resurrected. I knew God had used me to affect many more people's lives through my career at school. In the shower one morning, God asked me what my dream had been. I replied, "To look after and spend time with my family." All at once I had a light bulb moment. Anne, our eldest was due to return to teaching after Maternity leave in the coming September and I suddenly realised that if I retired, I could help her with childcare. I could hand on the baton for teaching, as it were, to her and enable her family to have the best possible circumstances for them all to get used to her working again. God fulfilled my dream as I looked after 1-year old Phoebe full-time for a year until she was 2 years old. I dropped off and picked up Zoë from school each day.

During the previous year, my elderly parents felt they needed more support, so we went up monthly to garden and did odd jobs for them, but it wasn't enough. They looked into moving into sheltered accommodation, going on quite a journey exploring this idea before deciding to stay where they were. We began to consider the possibility that we should move up there near them but weren't at peace about selling the house. Instead, we started to explore renting a property up in Peterborough.

There were two things we needed as confirmation. First, it would be good if Abi rented our house so that her dogs who were living with us wouldn't have to move. She was living elsewhere, so we needed a positive answer from her without putting her under undue pressure. Second, we needed furnished accommodation, as Abi would need a lot of our furniture if she moved back in.

Our search for furnished accommodation in my parent's local area came up empty. We then thought maybe there would be a family going abroad who wanted people to rent their property whilst they were away, so we asked Elaine's parents and any other contacts in different churches to put an advert in their churches' notice sheet. There was a strong sense from both of us that someone would have the answer to our prayer and that we would be the answer to their prayer. In January we gave God the deadline of mid-May to answer our prayers; if He didn't, we would have to start thinking about selling our house and moving permanently up there.

God, of course, had a plan all along!

By mid-May, Abi had said, "Yes" and a lady in my Mum and Dad's church had a bungalow, half a mile from their house which was perfect. We were the answer to her prayer, and she was the answer to ours. In September 2018, eighteen months before Coronavirus hit the world, we moved in. God knew that we needed to be settled near my Parents and Aunty during this crisis! Phil expanded his connections with churches to the East Anglia area, and I agreed to support Phil as a volunteer with OM. I'm now writing a children's book, one of the other dreams of my youth.

A NOTE FROM ANNE

After getting my degree in teaching at Bishop Grosseteste College, Lincoln, I went on to live in Worksop and teach for a year in the picturesque, rural village of Harthill, near Sheffield. I always knew there was a missionary calling on my life and often thought back to our visit to Constanta on the Black Sea where one of OM's ships, MV Doulos, was docked. We were fortunate enough to have a personal tour of the ship, and I can remember meeting one of the Primary school teachers on board who told me that there would be a need for a teacher in two years' time. Throughout the following two years, I often thought back to this comment and wondered, "What if?"

ANNE GRADUATION

This was to be one of my biggest challenges in trusting God for his plan for my future. I adored the little school where I worked in Harthill and had become part of the village community. I approached my headteacher to ask for advice and I clearly remember her saying to me, "Follow your heart, Anne."

I prepared to set off on my new adventure, with their blessing. They even held a sponsored skipping competition in the playground to raise money for my travels. As I planned and fundraised for the two-year experience, I often had doubts about whether I was doing the right thing. God continued to reassure me through moments of peace in my heart and confirmation from other people. I remember meeting a lady in the post office in Harthill one day. She handed me an envelope and said, "I think you might need this!" That lady had no idea of my plans and yet inside the envelope was a cheque for £1000, which was the amount that I needed to complete my fundraising. I was astonished, and this certainly was confirmation that I was following God's plan for my next steps.

I served onboard MV Doulos for two years as a teacher for Key Stage 1 children of different nationalities who lived with their parents on the ship. It was such an enriching experience and taught me how to become adaptable and flexible in a school environment. Only two children had English as their first language, which was a healthy challenge. My biggest schooling highlight was one of our trips to the jungle in Madagascar to see the lemurs. During my time on board, I grew in my faith deeply, learning to love others unconditionally (especially when sleeping in a four-person cabin for two years). I overcame many of my fears, knowing that even though I was on board one of the oldest ships in the world, floating in the middle of the ocean, I was safe and exactly where God wanted me.

It was in my last year, where I became good friends with Izwe (now my husband) who worked as an engineer and watchkeeper in the Engine Room. He inspired me with the way that he knew and quoted scriptures from the Bible and when he prayed, it was truly a special experience. We married on 2 August 2008, and then went on to have two precious daughters, Zoë (born in October 2010) and Phoebe (born

NKOSI FAMILY

in August 2016). Every day, I am surprised and amazed at the many talents and gifts that God has given to our children. It is strange to think that if I had not served on the Doulos and followed God's call, I probably would not have been so blessed in this way, perhaps.

I have continued my career in teaching and have been teaching at Parkside School in Cobham for the last twelve years - currently Head of the Middle School. We are members of Emmaus Rd Church in Guildford.

I wonder what our next adventure will be?

A NOTE FROM RACHEL

Since being in Romania for that year, I have now been nursing for fourteen years. Strangely enough, I ended back in Surrey. I specialised in cancer nursing training at the Marsden, then onto Palliative Care at a Hospice, which felt like a job literally designed for me. I loved my job, even with all the sadness and heartbreak of seeing people suffering through grief and loss.

RACHEL GRADUATION

After nursing, my next big adventure was moving to Athens in Greece in August 2019. I knew that as much as I loved my nursing and life in Surrey, supported by amazing friends and family, there was something more God wanted to do with my nursing. I felt called to start exploring Europe, specifically places with displaced people after seeing a news report on the thousands of refugees coming into Europe, living in difficult situations in camps, travelling for miles, escaping from situations that have forced them to leave their homes. After visiting a few countries, I came to Athens in Greece. Hearing God's call that it was right to come here to Greece was similar to hearing God's call to Romania. On my first visit to Athens, I went with my friend and mentor, Linda Harding. I was wondering if this was the place God had put on my heart. Linda asked a very simple but wise question, "Why not?" I couldn't come up with a good enough reason that didn't involve myself, security and comfort, so this question led to my second trip to Athens. It was on my second visit I knew this was a place that God would use me, with both my nursing skills and my heart for vulnerable people.

After eight months here, I can say that moving alone to another country as an adult has been a very different experience than as a teenager. I hadn't appreciated the amount my parents did arranging everything and dealing with the problems that came up frequently. I also missed not having the ready-made support of family around me,

RACHEL IN ATHENS

their humour and culture. It has taken time to settle, running into many frustrating cultural differences and at the same time being pleasantly surprised by the fast-growing warmth I feel towards the Greek people and those from other countries that I'm working with in Athens.

EPILOGUE

It's extraordinary that I'm reading back over what I wrote for this book so many years ago, including the description about me not learning well through books, but through being immersed in the culture and language. I was wondering why my intensive Greek university course for three hours a day in a class setting was causing me stress and frustration! Now I'm reminded why! Also, reading about the slow pace of Romania and having to change the speed at which things are done, is a timely reminder. In some ways, the Greek and Romanian culture are quite similar. My time in Romania definitely prepared me for Greece.

I am very grateful and thank God for His peace even in the times when I miss close friends and family; I have never felt I am in the wrong place. My heart for the people here continues to grow.

A NOTE FROM BECKY

I have now been in South East Asia for eight years, continuing to live amongst a people group who live high up in the Himalayas; doing everyday life with them and sharing the gifts of hope and peace that Jesus has given me.

This country is a place that truly provides an abundance of adventures. Life here is never boring. A desire for adventure and new

BECKY GRADUATION

experiences was definitely something that was birthed in me during our time in Romania, and the country I am living in now definitely give me enough excitement and surprises to keep me living life on the edge. It's also slow, raw and simple; aspects I have grown to appreciate.

There have been many hardships and suffering during this time. I have learnt to trust God on a deeper level, knowing He is unchanging and always in control even when I don't always understand His ways. I have continued journeying with the lesson of having home in God, and these tough times have deepened my longing for the heavenly home that is to come.

BECKY IN NEPAL

The longer I am here, the more years I become integrated into the culture. I'm aware that I will never be an insider, but instead of this disturbing me, I'm content knowing it is not meant to be my home.

The people I live among here are resilient, they are survivors. I have a deep respect for the way they naturally find the fun and joy in life, even when things are messy or not going to plan. They remind me of my family in Romania and the lessons I learnt from them to go with the flow, allow plans to be fluid, and find the fun in the mess of life. I long to return there one day, relive our memories and reconnect with the place and people who laid these significant bricks into the foundation of my life.

EPILOGUE

A NOTE FROM ABI

Currently, I work as a referral veterinary nurse at Fitzpatrick Referrals on night shifts. I have 2 Goldendoodles, Jasper (nearly 11 years old) and Charlie (nearly 3 years old).

Moving to a new country where you don't know the culture or language takes a massive step in faith; I relied on God that He would look after me. He blessed me with the ability to pick up Hungarian quickly and be able to translate for my dad, but what I didn't know was that it would also be useful for later in my life when I had to translate for my boss (the Supervet, Noel Fitzpatrick)! It's amazing how God uses us in unexpected ways.

I went off to university at the Royal Veterinary College. My experience in Romania, having Barney and calling daily to get the milk from the milk lady, made me passionate about nursing animals.

ABI GRADUATION

Having had Barney as my dog in Romania and being unable to bring him back to England, was tough. So again, I started on the route of trying to convince my parents to let me have another dog. It eventually worked and I got Jasper. Somehow, I managed to twist their arm again after 8 years and Charlie joined the clan.

As you have read, my family is very mission-focused and currently, I have two sisters who are serving abroad. People are always asking when it is my turn. Sometimes it gets me frustrated as it seems to be the expectation for our family. Having discussed it with God many times, He has made it clear that I am in the right place. My family describe me as the rock of the family, the one who can always be relied on for support from back home. I would never have dreamed of trekking in the Himalayas if Becky wasn't in Nepal, and I look forward to visiting Rach in Greece.

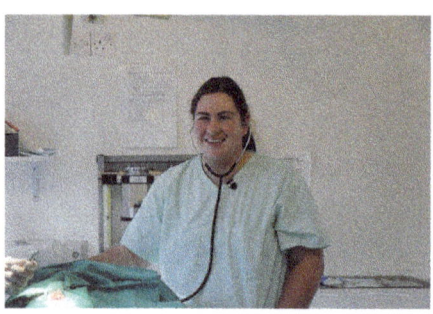

ABI AT WORK

I have loved our adventures as a family, and this has made our family so strong. I couldn't ask for a more amazing family, and I have learnt over my adventurous life that God is always faithful when we put our trust in Him.

Even though there are highs and lows, the experiences and knowledge that I gained during this time in Romania far outweighed the difficult times I experienced on my return. Even though the first two years back in England were tough, I would not have changed the opportunity of growing up in a different country and all that I learned about myself and God. If I had the choice, I would do it all over again.

EPILOGUE

A FINAL NOTE

So, what did The Head teacher at Therfield School say before we decided to go to Romania? "Grab the opportunity with both hands and that as long as you keep up with English and Maths, the education the girls will receive will be far and away richer than if they stay at Therfield!"

PHIL AT SZÉKELYKERESZTÚR

These accounts of our lives since Transylvania prove that God took care of the girls' education and their lives, as they were prepared for life and living on the edge.

Transylvania was a significant event in our family's life and was one of the foundation blocks for the girls' future lives. We have many, many stories of answered prayer, miracles and God-incidences over the rest of our lives which we often recall together. God has been faithful throughout our lives; we are ordinary people but with an extraordinary God!

OUR JOURNEY FROM THE UK TO ROMANIA

EPILOGUE

Image by FreePix (adapted)

www.ingramcontent.com/pod-product-compliance
Lightning Source LLC
Chambersburg PA
CBHW040415100526
44588CB00022B/2833